"Once we've learned the basics of Wiccan beliefs and practices, living our religion is, logically, the next step. How we allow it to affect our lives is completely up to us.

"I've written this book as a guide not only to Wiccan practice, but to Wiccan life. Still, its contents are merely ideas and suggestions. Each of us has to find the perfect path. May the Goddess and God assist you in this quest."

Scott Cunningham,
1956–1993

ABOUT THE AUTHOR

Scott Cunningham was born in Royal Oak, Michigan on June 27, 1956. He learned about Wicca while still in high school and practiced elemental magic for twenty years. He experienced, researched, then wrote about what he learned in his magical training. He then rewrote it, as many times as it took, to get it right by his high standards. Scott is credited with writing more than thirty books (both fiction and non-fiction). His style is simple and direct. He passed from this incarnation on March 28, 1993, but his work and his words live on.

About Llewellyn's Practical Magick Series

To some people, the idea that "Magick" is practical comes as a surprise.It shouldn't. The entire basis for Magick is to exercise influence over one's environment. Magick is an interactive process of spiritual growth and psychological transformation. Even so, the spiritual life rests firmly on material foundations. Magick is a way of life and must be lived, not just talked about, and that includes experiencing the wonders, pleasures and pains of material existence. The material world and the spiritual are intertwined and it is this very interconnectedness that provides the Magickal Link, the magickal means for the spirit to influence the material, and vice versa.

Magick can be used in one's daily life for better living and in opening the doors to new worlds of mind and spirit. Each of us has been given Mind and Body, and it is our spiritual opportunity to make full use of these wonderful gifts. Mind and Body work together, and Magick is simply the extension of this interaction into dimensions beyond the limits normally perceived. That's why we commonly talk of the "supernormal" in connection with the domain of Magick.

The Body is alive, and all Life is an expression of the Divine. There is spiritual, Magickal power in the Body and in the Earth, just as there is in Mind and spirit. With Love and Will, we use Mind to link these aspects of Divinity together to bring about change. We add to the beauty of it all—for to work Magick we must work in concert with the Laws of Nature and of the Psyche. *Magick is the flowering of our Human Potential.*

Practical Magick is concerned with the Craft of living well, in harmony with the cycles of Nature and the seasons of the Earth. We increase the flow of Divinity in our lives, and in the world around us, through the things we make with hand and mind. All our acts of Will and desire are magickal acts.

LLEWELLYN'S PRACTICAL MAGICK SERIES

Living Wicca

A FURTHER GUIDE FOR THE SOLITARY PRACTITIONER

SCOTT CUNNINGHAM

1996
Llewellyn Publications
St. Paul, MN 55164-0383, U.S.A.

Cover Art: Robin Wood
Cover Design: Chris Wells
Book Design: Kelly Bell

FIRST EDITION
Sixth Printing, 1996

Library of Congress Cataloging-in-Publications Data

Cunningham, Scott,   1956 – 1993
     Living wicca : a further guide for the solitary practitioner /
Scott Cunningham.
          p.   cm. — (Llewellyn's practical magick series)
     Includes bibliographical references and index.
     ISBN 0–87542–184–9
     1. Witchcraft.   2. Magic.   3. Ritual.   I. Title.   II. Series.
BF1566.C84 1993
133.4'3—dc20   93–24673
                                                                        CIP

Llewellyn Publications
A Division of Llewellyn Worldwide, Ltd.
P.O. Box 64383, St. Paul, MN 55164-0383

This book is dedicated to
Solitary Wiccans
everywhere

TABLE OF CONTENTS

PART 3: YOUR OWN TRADITION

A NOTE TO
'TRADITIONAL' WICCANS

This book, a further guide for Solitary practitioners of Wicca, isn't an attack on conventional Wicca, Wiccan traditions, covens or usual training procedures. It was written (as was its predecessor) for those without access to conventional Wicca, Wiccan traditions, covens or usual training procedures.

Some will see this book as an insult to their form of Wicca, so I repeat: this is a guide for Solitary practitioners who have no access to your form of Wicca. This in no way lessens it or any other Wiccan tradition.

Read with an open mind and remember the time when you, too, were seeking.

INTRODUCTION

This book consists of further instructions for the Solitary Wiccan Practitioner. It assumes that the reader has gained some experience in our religion and, thus, doesn't stop to define every specialized term and ritual reference. For a quick review, check the glossary.

Part I of this book contains essays on a variety of topic of importance or interest to Solitary Wiccans. Part II is a collection of daily prayers and rituals of offering and thanks, together with guides to effective prayer and magic. Part III is a recommended system for creating your own Wiccan tradition.

This book has been written with a single premise: that Wicca is an open religion. All can come before the altar and worship the Goddess and God, whether alone or in the company of others; initiated or not. Wicca is available to all interested people.

Living Wicca has been written for those who have become enchanted by the moon shining through trees; who have begun to investigate the sublime world that lies out beyond the fabric of daily life, and who stand in smoke-shrouded circles, raising aloft their hands to greet the Goddess and God as the candles flicker on the altar. It's written for those of us who, through choice or circumstance, meet with Silver Lady and the Horned God alone.

Readers of *Wicca: A Guide for the Solitary Practitioner* asked me to write another, similar work, because so little Wiccan writing is aimed at the solitary practitioner. I hope that this book fills at least part of this need.

Until next time, I'll say Blessed Be.

Scott Cunningham
La Mesa, CA
July 10, 1992

PART ONE:

LEARNING

1: TOOLS OF LEARNING

Members of covens have access to teachers, attend learning circles, and can enjoy the experience of other Wiccans in guiding and enriching their Wiccan knowledge. Solitary Wiccans lack all of these opportunities. What, then, are our tools of learning?

We must be creative. Self-teaching is a great challenge, but it can be accomplished through the use of four tools:

Study

Thought

Prayer

Experimentation

The use of these tools is the most effective method by which Solitary Wiccans can increase their knowledge and understanding of Wicca. This four-fold approach may answer nearly every question you have if you're willing to trust yourself; if you're willing to think; and if you're not caught up in worrying that you're doing something incorrectly.

There's no one correct method of casting a circle; of invoking the Goddess and God; of ritually observing the seasons or performing Wiccan magic. The fact that there are numerous methods of casting circles, invoking the Goddess and God and observing the seasons points to the unique opportunity that lies in wait for the Solitary Wiccan: to discover new forms of worship that others, conditioned to accept only certain avenues of Wiccan expression, may have missed.

How can you do this? By studying, thinking, praying and experimenting.

STUDY

Books have always been tools of magic. With the turn of a page, we can be transported to the bottom of the ocean; to the limitless desert; to the surface of the moon. Books can lift our spirits, heal our wounds, steel our courage and strengthen our religious resolve. They can also arouse our curiosity, sharpen our minds, teach us new skills and alter our opinions. Books are powerful tools of change.

Many people first learn of Wicca through reading books, and most use books to guide their first steps on the Wiccan path. Such books, if written in a clear manner by experienced Wiccans, can be valuable learning tools. Quality books of this kind become their readers' High Priestess and High Priest, coveners and friends.

Indeed, due to the scarcity of those willing to teach Wicca, and the small number of students that they can effectively instruct, we've thrown the mantle of experience and authority around books written by Wiccan authors. Such works have largely become the teachers of the new era of Wicca.

Sometimes, however, reading more than a few books may lead to confusion. Authors may make contradictory statements regarding Wiccan ritual practices and concepts. Some may deliberately obscure Wiccan knowledge with mystic prose. The Solitary Wiccan, grasping for answers, may only come up with more questions, as expert after expert states that her or his way is the best or most effective (this tendency is disappearing in Wiccan books today, but many older books that contain such statements are still in print).

One book may state, "the altar is always in the East"; in another, the North. An author might write that counterclockwise movement within the circle is forbidden; another will direct the reader to move in precisely this direction. Dates and names for the Sabbats and Esbats vary widely according to the author. Tools are given differing names, attributes and functions.

Eventually, the books that originally inspired the new Solitary Wiccan may become a source of confusion and despair, and she or he may pack them away, deciding that no real learning can be achieved with them.

This is a shame, and can be avoided by keeping this concept in mind: Each book is a different teacher. Each teacher has distinct ideas concerning the subject being taught. Think of four experienced race-car drivers who are teaching beginners. Each instructs his or her student in the basics of this dangerous sport. The fastest engine designs; the best oil; the most effective strategy to use during the races themselves. Each driver teaches this subject in a different way, and expresses her or his biases, but they're all teaching racing.

Wiccan books, as teachers, are quite similar. Experience and training have created specific ideals concerning Wicca within each book's writer, and these ideals are clearly presented within her or his books. Divergences of opinion are natural in experts in any field and shouldn't dismay those who are confronted by them.

When you're challenged with seemingly contradictory information, examine this information and make a decision as to which to follow. Listen to your intuition. In other words, feel free to pick and choose among the published rituals and ritual textbooks to decide what *feels* right. It's this selectivity that will usually prove to be the most effective.

I can already hear some of you saying: "Wait! I could never do that! I – I wouldn't know if I was doing it right. I need someone to teach me!"

That's where you come in. You become your own teacher, and books provide some of the lessons. Learn to trust yourself. Settle questions in the best way that you can. Think. Pray. Experiment (see the next three sections of this chapter). And just do it.

Books aren't foolproof. Some books contain virtually no accurate information. Many readers are apt to believe anything in print. "After all," they say, "it's in this book right here. That proves it's true." Unfortunately, nearly anyone can write a book and even have it published. Does this ensure that its contents are true?

No. In fact, a few specialty publishers continue to publish lie-packed books describing the 'Satanic' nature of Wicca; that describe its rites as those of human sacrifice, orgies and prayers to the Devil. Such books, written by a few virulent self-styled Christians, are easily spotted among others on the shelves by the repeated use of Biblical quotations. These hateful tomes have nothing to teach and are best avoided.

Other books, while written by scholars or others intersected in accurately recording Wiccan beliefs and practices, may contain misinformation. Most surveys of Wiccan belief (such as by Tanya Luhrman's *Persuasions of the Witches' Craft*) are so slanted by the author's bias that little truth has managed to squeeze onto their pages. Again, it's best to avoid books of this nature and all books written by non-Wiccans about Wicca.

Another pitfall that may be encountered within books consists of glowing descriptions of negative magic. Such passages are usually found in spell books, not in Wiccan texts. Still, Solitary Wiccans are apt to peruse magical texts, and the majority of these describe the wonders of cursing and reveal numerous methods of hexing one's enemies. Such books may otherwise contain fine information, but passages like these can perpetuate the false idea that negative magic is acceptable. Material of this nature can be weeded out by a simple recitation of the Wiccan Law: *Harm none.*

Finally, some older books by Wiccans contain what seem to be absolute statements of fact that are absolutely false, such as "Wicca is a British religion"; "You must be naked in your rites"; "Sexual rites are necessary in Wicca", or our old friend, "Only a Witch can make a Witch" (i.e., initiation is necessary). These statements are framed within the context of these authors' Wiccan traditions, and may be quite correct within them. However, they have no validity to those outside their tradition. Such statements, where they appear in books, needn't concern us.

One of the most popular forms of misinformation concerning Wicca are found in books on the ancient history of Wicca. I won't add to this argument, but I will advise you to read tales of ancient Wicca with a great deal of discernment and a large grain of salt.

While books aren't infallible sources of information, they can be valuable allies on the Solitary Path if you keep these things in mind:

- Books are tools that are meant to be used. They provide lessons; we have to put the lessons to work.

- Books can't answer every question, but neither can any High Priestess or teacher.

- Be discriminating when reading books. If an author makes wild statements that you know to be untrue, consider the book as a *possible* source of incorrect information.

- Mark up your books. Underline (with pencils) important passages, or use bookmarks to indicate valuable sections. You may wish to add to the index (many Wiccans do this). (Purists may purchase a second copy of the same book and leave this one in pristine condition on the shelf.)

- Combine information from a number of books on a specific topic, such as magic, energy raising or circle construction. Write notes and study the combined teachings of several books. This may facilitate the process of assimilating (and using) this information, and will give you a greater chance of finding what's right for you. (This process of collecting information, combining it and utilizing it is one of the most important parts of learning any new skill, profession, hobby or religion.) (See Part III of this book.)

⊙ If books are too expensive for your budget, budget differently, or haunt used book stores in your area. Libraries are another possible source of Wiccan books, but don't expect to find them on the shelf: they're usually stolen if openly shelved. Most libraries keep occult books behind the counter or in storage. Some librarians may look with disgust at you for checking out books on Wicca. If this is a problem, say you're working on a paper, ask the person if she or he has a problem, or simply say nothing and stare down the librarian. (Actually, most librarians don't care what books are checked out.)

⊙ Finally, don't see reading as a passive activity. Make it an active process in which you play a vital role. Question everything, even this book and these instructions. Think about what you're learning (see next section). Never take an author at her or his word. Search for similar themes. Remember 'harm none'. Books are wonderful teachers, but we must allow ourselves to hear their messages and trust ourselves so that their lessons can begin to unfold.

THOUGHT

I've already mentioned the importance of independent thought during study. This thought process should continue after you've closed the book. Many Wiccan teachers state that the classes that they lead are just the beginning of the lesson; that they should be springboards to continual learning. This can take place only when we reflect upon what we're being taught.

This is in direct opposition to the 'think this way, believe this way' attitude of most educational systems in this country. Independent thought thrusts a stick into the spokes of conventional education, and is seen as a real threat to the old order. It's discourages at any but the highest levels of education and in the most obscure disciplines (Masters degree programs; medical research; physics and so on).

Thought is often combined with questioning. The question initiates (pardon the pun) the learning process. "How do I make a magic circle?" can be answered by reading, then reflecting on what's been learned. This thought process *must* follow the uncovering of new information if it is to be available for use as needed.

Thinking through new material (such as various methods of casting the circle) allows you to closely examine it to weed out unsatisfactory information. If a published athame consecration leaves you cold, or requires two people, you can easily place it in the inactive file of your mind. Thus, thinking about what you've learned is part of the process of elimination, and of finding your ideal Wiccan practice. It's an integral aspect of the learning process.

Everything stated above applies equally to questions regarding the nature of the Goddess and God, reincarnation, morality and every other aspect of Wiccan belief and practice.

Many new Solitary Wiccans have a great number of questions regarding the Goddess: "What does She look like?", "What's the best method of contacting Her?"; "Is She really real?"; "Can I touch Her?"; "Where did She come from?"; "Which myths should I use?" Many of these and similar questions can be answered through study and thought; others require prayer and experimentation.

Thought should also be combined with *feeling*. We've been taught to distrust our feelings. In Wicca, however, we can realize that our feelings are usually what attracted us to Wicca in the first place. Would it be wise to toss them aside. I don't think so.

Intuition (the unexplained knowledge or feeling that makes itself known in our conscious minds) is a form of psychic awareness. Use of this tool while learning Wicca is of the utmost importance, for it's the filter through which you can evaluate questionable information. Your reactions to this information may profoundly affect your final decisions.

Thought, then, is a necessary part of learning Solitary Wicca. It can be summed in the following manner:

- Determine questions (if necessary).

- Study to uncover knowledge.

- Determine your feelings concerning this knowledge. Rely on your intuition.

- Based on this, determine what information is applicable to your Solitary Wiccan practice.

Such processes are necessary for Solitary Wiccans. Reflect on what you've studied. Trust yourself, your intuition, your feelings. And learn.

PRAYER

Prayer is another tool open to the Wiccan. When you're absolutely stuck, when the information can't be found in books, or when found confuses you. When you have a real need for assistance, ask for it. Prayer of this nature needn't be accompanied by lengthy ritual (particularly if you haven't yet determined your best ritual forms). You might accompany your prayer with the lighting of a candle or a walk in the woods or park. You may pray while petting your cat, staring into a fire, standing in a shower or sinking into a tub. You might also use a popular tool of divination, such as tarot cards, a pendulum, rune stones, but use such tools *following* prayer – not before.

The structure of the prayer isn't as important as the emotion that you place within it, and the clarity of your request. You might direct it solely to the Goddess or to both the Goddess and the God. Express your need for this information or for guidance with the present situation, and thank Them in advance for Their assistance.

True prayer is more than spoken words, for the devotee releases energy through the prayer to the Goddess and God. Because nature abhors a vacuum, an answer will appear (see Chapter 8 for more information regarding Wiccan prayer).

This answer may take many forms. It can be something as simple as a voice suddenly saying, "I have much to teach you. Place two candles on the altar. Hold Sabbats at night after everyone else is asleep. You need not initiate yourself at this time. Wine is fine, but apple cider or grape juice can also be used." Such direct communication with the Goddess is possible because we each contain a spark of Her divine fire within us. However, such direct communication is rather rare.

More commonly, the messages may appear in symbolic form: a cloud may suggest a shape; the shape may suggest an answer. Cards or stones or the movement of a pendulum could give you answers. Prayers for information before going to sleep might be answered in dreams. Record all such important dreams, think about them and determine if they're relevant to your question. (During sleep, communication with the Goddess and God is much easier, for the doubting conscious mind has been unchained and we operate in the subconscious [psychic] mind.)

There are numerous other ways in which your prayer may be answered. You may suddenly find a book that contains the needed information, or come across an article in a Wiccan publication that's just arrived in the mail. Prayers are always answered, but not always in direct ways.

Keep in mind, however, that the answers you receive may not be relevant for anyone but yourself. If the Goddess has spoken to you, it is to you that She has spoken – not to all Wiccans. Her messages may have little or no meaning to others. If you've always been fascinated by semi-precious stones and She tells you to create a circle with them, this knowledge is correct for you but may be completely incorrect for others. Divine revelations are usually of a personal, not global, nature. Though knowledge received in this fashion certainly should be used, it doesn't invalidate the ways of other Wiccans. Though we may receive divine messages, no one can ever be *the* spokesperson for the Goddess.

Answers received in prayer deserve attention and thanks (rites of thanks to the Goddess and God can be found in Chapter 10).

Don't discount prayer as a tool of information gathering. It seems ethereal, but when we consider its source, is this so surprising?

EXPERIMENTATION

So, you've read many books, thought about what you've read and compiled information from a number of sources; you've filtered this knowledge through the sieve of your feelings (intuition) and have prayed to the deities for assistance. What's next? Putting the information into practice.

Wicca is, after all, a living religion. Religions don't exist within theories and ritual plans; they come to life only when they're being practiced and lived. The outer forms (rituals, uses of tools) are important because they symbolize non-physical processes, and remind us of what we're doing in Wicca in the first place.

Begin to experiment with various ritual forms. Piece them together in various ways, discarding unsuccessful combinations and holding onto those that you find fulfilling. Questions such as "Is this the right way? Am I doing it wrong?" should not be allowed to interfere with your creative process. Such questions will only delay your progress.

The process of experimentation is necessary for determining all aspects of Solitary Wicca: everything from seasonal festivals to Esbats, power raising and sending techniques, magical rituals, the use and meaning of tools, self-initiations and every other exterior aspect of Wicca.

✪   ✪   ✪

This four step self-learning plan can certainly be of value in sharpening your Wiccan beliefs and practices. How important is reincarnation in your Wiccan practice? How far can the law 'harm none' be taken? When's the best time to perform rituals? Do you have to hold a circle on every full moon and Sabbat? Can you do them at other times as well? Each of these questions can be answered through study, thought, prayer and experimentation.

A complete guide to creating your own Solitary Wiccan Tradition and writing your own *Book of Shadows* can be found in Part III of this book. The information in that chapter should be useful if you decide to take this step.

You may decide that none of this is necessary. You might find a set of rituals and follow them to the exclusion of any others. This, too, is fine. But when you have questions about these rituals you may wish to use the process outlined in this chapter to discover the answers.

The path of the Solitary Wiccan can be difficult, but the school of trial and error is an excellent one. As your experience increases, so will your knowledge, and so too will your questions, which will lead to *study, thought, prayer* and *experimentation*.

Having access to all the answers isn't the goal of the Solitary Wiccan – finding the most important of those answers is; and we can find them by practicing our religion and though the use of these tools of learning.

2 : SECRECY

Secrecy has been granted such importance in both Wicca and magic that a few words concerning it here seem appropriate. In this chapter, we'll separately discuss each topic.

KEEPING YOUR WICCAN ACTIVITIES SECRET

In the recent past, when there were far fewer members of our religion and public understanding of Pagan faiths was non-existent in this country, Wiccans were usually quiet about their religion. The threat of broken marriages, loss of home, job, and even children was quite real. Wiccans had learned to keep their religious activities wrapped in the shadows. Only the closest of relatives or friends knew what these people did on the nights of the full moon (and the reason why they always asked for the day off after the Sabbats).

These Wiccans were usually members of covens and had been sworn to secrecy during their initiations. Among the many things that they could not reveal were their magical names, the identities of other members of the coven, activities that occurred during a circle, and their group's specific religious and magical rituals. Even if some Wiccans were willing to speak of their religion, public opinion and oaths of secrecy were stacked against them. Most Wiccans lived double lives: one related to work, PTA, fighting with the neighbors, budgeting, washing the car and other mundane activities; the other immersed in religion and magic.

Today, the picture has somewhat changed. Every issue of *Circle Net-work News* (see the Appendix) lists a large number of positive articles that have appeared concerning Wicca in general-interest magazines and news-papers. Articles on Wiccans and Goddess-worshippers have appeared on the front page of the *Wall Street Journal*. Television talk shows revel in 'Witch' episodes, where invited Wiccans discuss their religion.

This coverage has tremendously expanded the awareness of the exis-tence of our religion within non-Wiccans. They may have incorrect ideas concerning Wicca, but they've been exposed to its existence.

Recognized Wiccans are sometimes invited to speak to church congre-gations to explain their religion. Many work directly with prisoners, just as do the clergy of other religions. Some Wiccan groups are recognized by the I.R.S. as tax-exempt churches (though Wicca as a whole hasn't been granted this recognition). The U.S. Army instructs its chaplains to recog-nize Wicca as a legitimate alternative religion. Occasionally, articles about Wicca actually appear in the Religion section of newspapers.

Still, the prevailing climate is one of confusion, doubt and fear. Those raised to believe in one faith feel threatened when another makes its presence known; especially one as misunderstood as Wicca. Occasionally, this leads to violence and even murder.

Such reactions are the direct result of the misinformation continually being fed to an unsuspecting public. The major sources of these lies are television evangelists (who have had their day and who are now fading from existence), but many small-town preachers continue to speak of us as satanic, child-killing devils with one aim: to rule the world. Even the recent media-promulgated "New Age" has been widely discussed as a satanic threat to Christianity.

Though we know this is absurd, many non-Wiccans do not. In such a heady climate, is it best to reveal your religion to your parents, mate, children, friends, employers, landlords and neighbors? If only to some of these, which ones? Could such a revelation create anger, fear and misunderstanding to the point that you wished you'd never said a thing?

It's possible. The alternative is also possible. Telling your mate that you're practicing a different religion may actually strengthen your bond ("Well, at least you believe in *something*") or settle unresolved questions ("So *that's* what you've been doing at midnight once a month").

The alternative is true as well. Your mate may grow cold, your employer may let you go, your neighbors might shun you, your parents may become extremely distressed (if they subscribe to a more conventional religion), your landlord may give you 30 days notice, or up your rent.

An understanding employer might let you have days off for your religious practices. Your neighbors will know not to drop in on the nights of the full moon. Your landlord? Well, maybe it's best not to tell everyone. You must carefully weigh this decision, for such a revelation could quickly affect your place of residence.

The decision of if and when to break the news to others, and to whom, must be based upon your knowledge of Wicca, your involvement in the religion (after a while, it can become rather difficult to hide), your relationships with those you might tell, the prevailing religious climate of your area, and the ease with which you can discuss such a highly personal subject as religion.

It usually isn't necessary to make such a revelation, not even to your husband or wife. If she or he asks, you may wish to discuss it, but no one has the right to know what you do on October 31. Religious freedom is just that—freedom of religion, freedom from oppressive religions, and the freedom from discussing your faith.

For 13 years I lived in a second floor apartment in a rough neighborhood. The building was owned by a born-again Christian who ran a gun shop and vacuum cleaner repair business next door to the building. I saw this man on a daily basis; he was in my apartment many times, and I had met much of his family. While I lived there I had 10 magic and Wiccan books published, gave countless television, radio and newspaper interviews, taught hundreds of classes in the general area, performed many rituals and hosted dozens of coven meetings. I stared at the stars at night, recited incantations over the herbs and plants that I grew on my porch, meditated on thunderstorms and in every way acted as a Wiccan.

And yet, during all those years my landlord never spoke to me about my religion. Yes, he used to write rent receipts on the back of religious tracts, but the subject simply never came up. I held my tongue, he held his, and we had a satisfying business relationship.

If I'd marched into his store one day and announced that I was a Witch, he'd have certainly sent me packing. My decision not to discuss my religion allowed me to live in a large apartment, at low rent, for a great many years during my salad days as a writer.

The decision of whether to inform others of your Wiccanhood must be a personal one. However, I'll give you a warning: many people simply don't care what you believe or who you invoke. They have no interest in the subject.

Some Wiccans decide to tell the world that they're Wiccans (or 'Witches') purely for shock value, to attract attention, make money and to gratify their egos. This is the worst reason for revealing your religion to others.

MAGICAL SECRECY

Virtually everything said above also pertains to the practice of magic, but other factors are pertinent only to this subject. Magic, as the projection of natural energies to manifest needed changes, is a vital part of Wicca. Within the circle we send energy to our planet, assist in healing the sick, protect ourselves, draw love into our lives and plant the seeds for many changes.

Magic can be a daily activity. Many Wiccans practice folk magic, the creation of charms and enchanted herbal mixtures, the use of stones and other natural, energy-filled objects to create needed change. These changes may be minor or, at times, quite major. Folk magic usually isn't practiced inside the circle itself. This section will discuss secrecy for both ritual and folk magic.

It's commonly believed that secrecy is absolutely essential for successful magic. Don't speak of your magical workings, we're told. Don't tell your friends of your interest in magic, let alone discuss the candle ritual that you performed last night. Be still, we're told. Talk not. Let the power cook.

A few reasons are given for this magical secrecy. Some say that speaking of your magical operations disperses the energies that you've put into them. Others state that non-magicians who hear of your rituals will, by simply disbelieving in magic, unconsciously send energies that will block your spell's manifestation. A few Wiccans will state that secrecy about one's magical proclivities was once a necessity for saving one's neck. (This is certainly true.) For a very few, secrecy heightens the mysterious quality of magic. Others give no reason, but simply repeat the old code: "Be silent."

Is this superstition? Perhaps. Magic is still a somewhat uncertain practice. After all, we're using energies that even physicists haven't yet been able to locate or identify. We may have seen the effectiveness of our magical rituals. We may have even told a few close friends about these rituals prior to their manifestations, with no ill effects. But soon, the secrecy issue could creep back into our consciousness.

"Should I talk about these things?" some will ask. "After all, that book stated that loose lips sink spells. A Wiccan I know does rituals all the time, but she only tells me about them after they've taken effect. And I'm sure that there are lots of Wiccans who never breathe a word about their magical rites."

Doubt soon clouds the Solitary Wiccan's mind. Soon, she or he makes no mention of magic to others, even others of like mind. Secrecy has once again been conferred on the process.

This is unfortunate and unnecessary. True magic is limitless. Speaking of a ritual to others doesn't disperse its energies. On the contrary, it gives you another opportunity to quickly send more power toward your magical goal.

Disbelief also isn't a satisfactory reason for magical secrecy. The disbelief of others has as much effect on magic as does an unschooled person's doubt that a calculator can add 2 and 2 to equal 4. The calculator will work, regardless of the observer's doubt. So, too, will magic.

There are other possible reasons why the calculator won't perform this simple operation: faulty microchips; low battery power or a lack of batteries; an operator who pushes the incorrect buttons, or a button turned off. Still, observer's disbelief alone can't be the cause. The same is true of magic. Properly performed, magic will be effective. If energy is raised within the body, programmed with intent, and projected toward its goal with the proper force and visualization, it will be effective.

This manifestation may not occur overnight. Many repetitions of the magical ritual may be necessary, but they're usually effective if the Wiccan knows how to use this process.

Secrecy concerning magical rites is quite limiting and, indeed, can *reduce* their effectiveness. This is a bizarre statement, so I'd better explain.

If a person truly feels that secrecy is necessary to perform an effective rite of magic, she or he has accepted a limitation concerning magic's effectiveness. Acceptance of any form of limitation in magic reduces the Wiccan's ability to raise and send energy, for it breeds doubt within the

Wiccan's mind that magic isn't an all-powerful force that, correctly performed by properly experienced people, can truly manifest wondrous, positive changes.

Limitations (such as secrecy) are harmful to the effective practice of magic—both ritual and folk. If we accept one limitation, we may accept others that we either read in books or hear from others. (Examples include: You can't perform a positive ritual during the waning moon. You *must* check the lunar phase prior to performing any ritual. If you incorrectly time it, the ritual will flop. You have to have every single ingredient listed in a folk magic spell, for substitution of one item for another will render it void. There are many others – all are absurd.)

The third reason often proffered for magical secrecy, that it's a tradition handed down from earlier times when secrecy was necessary to save one's neck, is at least historically accurate. Fortunately, speaking of magical rituals to close friends today isn't likely to cause you to be hanged. The last rationale, that secrecy increases the mysterious nature of magic, may be necessary for some in the beginning of their magical experiences. They should soon lose the need for such mental stage settings.

Secrecy, then, isn't a necessary part of magic. It's no guarantee of magical success and may block your magic. This doesn't mean that you should walk around wearing a green button that states, "I did a money ritual last night!" It also doesn't mean that you *must* discuss your magical affairs with others, especially if you're working on intensely private matters.

It's perfectly fine to keep quiet concerning your magical activities – so long as your motivations aren't limiting. If you don't wish to discuss your magical activities with others, don't. Not because some Wiccan wrote that you shouldn't but because you don't want to.

Secrecy concerning magic is filled with superstition that has no place in the lives of Solitary Wiccans.

3: SHOULD I DO IT WHILE I'M SICK?

The question (do sickness and Wiccan ritual mix?) that entitles this chapter is an important one, yet is rarely mentioned in Wiccan books. Why? Information of this nature is usually provided by the High Priestess, High Priest or another experienced Wiccan. This is the type of question that usually doesn't pop up until the student is suffering through a cold or is taking a prescribed, powerful medication. The subject is so important (and so completely neglected in Wiccan literature) that it deserves a chapter within these pages.

When many Solitaries begin practicing Wicca, they hate to skip rituals for any reason, including sickness. Many coven members feel the same way. Is this wise?

Many types of illnesses create dramatic changes within humans. Some of these changes are physical; others are mental, emotional, spiritual or psychic. Are such temporary alterations beneficial or detrimental to the performance of Wiccan ritual?

These questions can be partially answered by an examination of illnesses and their effects. All information here pertains solely to religious Wiccan ritual and is generalized – you must use your own judgment.

Be attentive to your body. It usually knows what's best. Forcing yourself to perform Wiccan rituals while facing challenging illnesses and conditions can be dangerous. (For information on performing magic during sickness, see the end of this chapter.)

ILLNESS AND WICCAN RELIGIOUS RITUAL

PHYSICAL CHANGES

The physical aspects of sickness are usually the most obvious, so we'll begin here. Some illnesses create a pronounced lack of energy. It may be difficult to walk across the room, let alone cast a circle. In such a case, a ritual with limited physical activity is clearly indicated.

Casts on broken feet, hands, arms and other limbs may or may not restrict your ability to set up an altar and hold a Book of Shadows. At least in doing so you won't further endanger your health. Your movements in the circle, however, may have to be limited, so avoid slavishly following ritual directions. Adapt them to take into account your present physical condition.

If your health care practitioner has ordered bed rest, or told you to stay off your feet, follow her or his instructions. Either adapt ritual to a purely verbal and mental experience, or wait until you've recovered.

MENTAL CHANGES

During many types of sickness (including colds), a pronounced change of consciousness often occurs. Slight dizziness, sinus pressure, elevated temperature, pain and other symptoms can create the most remarkable shifts in consciousness—even in people who haven't attempted to mask the symptoms with drugs. This type of consciousness can lend the ill Wiccan a radically different perception of the world; one which usually hinders ritual work.

If you're staggering around and can't seem to concentrate, it's best to avoid working with magical knives, flames, incense and other potentially dangerous magical tools. If you're apt to 'space out' (that is, become mesmerized by objects, fall asleep or completely forget what you're doing), it's best to simply sit or lie comfortably and do little else. You might whisper a prayer to the Goddess and/or God, meditate upon an image, or perhaps draw a symbol and concentrate on it.

If you simply can't concentrate long enough to formulate any type of ritual, it's probably best to let it go for now and to resume ritual workings when you're once again able to do so.

EMOTIONAL AND SPIRITUAL CHANGES

Let's face it—most of us don't feel good when we're sick. We may be grumpy, irritable, impossible to be around, depressed, worried and stressed. Such emotional shifts often make us think, "Why bother doing ritual at all? I feel so bad I'll probably just blow it." Sometimes we're simply not in the mood. This is quite natural, and if you truly don't feel like doing ritual, don't. No one's keeping score.

On the other hand, if you're physically able to do so, performing ritual may actually make you feel better. Effective Wiccan ritual (which can be difficult to achieve during times of illness) gives us a spiritual boost, which in turn makes us feel better.

Finally, simple prayer to the Goddess and God may comfort you and if nothing else, give you a different focus than that of your illness.

PSYCHIC CHANGES

Illness can have great effects on our psychic awareness. Though this may not seem to be particularly important when doing rituals, our ability to tap into our psychic minds (psychic awareness) is necessary for effective ritual. Ritual is often empty and mechanical without this linking of the two minds (conscious and psychic).

You may possess the ability to physically, mentally and emotionally perform a Wiccan ritual, but if you seem to be psychically shut down (a difficult condition to describe that's immediately recognizable when it occurs), ritual probably wouldn't be a good idea.

NON-PRESCRIPTION AND PRESCRIPTION DRUGS

Drug reactions are perhaps the most important factor in determining whether to perform Wiccan rituals during illness. The vast number of such drugs now in use and their varying effects on their takers make it impossible to speak in any but the most general of terms.

Many drugs have no effect on consciousness, don't alter the emotions, have no noticeable physiological effect, and leave the psychic mind alone. However, some drugs (prescription and over-the-counter) can cause just these changes. Among these are, of course, narcotics. If you seem to be suffering from these or other negative side effects, limit ritual work while under their influence.

You must use your judgment and common sense in determining whether illness or prescription drugs will interfere with your Wiccan ritual. If your health care provider has told you to stay in bed, stay in bed and forget about setting up a circle. If you've just had stitches, don't do an ecstatic dance to the Goddess around the altar, no matter how much you may wish to do so. If you're suffering from lung complaints, don't burn incense. If you're taking a medication that prohibits alcohol use, don't drink wine after ritual. Solitary Wiccans can do ritual at any time and, if necessary, delay or miss ritual as well. Illness is a quite legitimate reason for skipping ritual.

Don't believe that you won't be a true Wiccan if you can't carry a candle around the circle on Imbolc because you're confined to your bed. Missing a ritual due to illness, infirmity or the influence of prescription drugs in no way makes you a lesser Wiccan. In fact, such a decision proves your intelligence and growing Wiccan experience: you've chosen to avoid performing what would most probably be a ritual lacking in energy and true contact with the Goddess and God. If this makes you a lesser Wiccan, I'll eat my cauldron.

MAGIC AND ILLNESS

Performing magic during periods of illness may or may not be a positive action. It's a natural time for self-healing spells, but spells for other reasons should be postponed, no matter how important the work may be. Waiting until you're well not only allows you to give the magical rite your full attention, it also assures that you'll be able to raise far greater amounts of energy.

When we're sick, our bodies have lowered reserves of energy (personal power). Not only aren't we producing as much as usual, we're also using more energy for healing ourselves. Less energy is available for any other physical task, including magic. This lowered reserve can make performing magic during serious illness quite dangerous, for you're drawing on the energy that would otherwise be working to heal you. This may extend the duration of your illness or slow the healing of wounds.

Willingly giving of this energy to solve someone else's problems is a good and noble deed—at any other time. When you're sick, you must be number one. Use this energy to heal yourself. Later, you'll be in shape to take care of the rest of the world.

The bottom line: no magic except self-healing during illness.

4: MAGICAL NAMES

Many Wiccan books discuss the taking of a Wiccan (magical) name. The ceremonial bestowing of such a name upon the initiate is a part of many initiation ceremonies. Afterward, the new Wiccan is usually exclusively called by this name within the circle.

Magical names are quite popular among Wiccans; so popular, in fact, that many Wiccans have two or even three such names: a public Craft name (used at Wiccan gatherings, when writing articles, and so on); a secret name (the one bestowed during initiation), and perhaps even a third name which is used only when addressing the Goddess and God, and is known only to Them and the Wiccan. Wiccans who are members of more than one tradition may have different names for each group.

For many Wiccans, taking a new name is an outward symbol of her or his devotion to Wicca. It's seen as a part of the process of rebirth into the religion.

Throughout history, names have been given considerable magical importance. A spirit's name had to be known before it could be exorcised from a sick person in ancient Sumer, Babylon and Assyria. In Hawaii, babies were given revolting names in infancy to guard them from molestation from evil during their early, vulnerable years. A more fitting name was given to the child when she or he reached a certain age and was less susceptible to the wiles of evil spirits. In some cultures, mothers will bestow a secret name on their children. This 'real' name, unknown to anybody but the mother, protects the child. The common name by which he or she is called has no power over them.

In our own country, numerology is used to discover the power of our names, and many people change their names to advance in their careers.

With all this importance attached to names, it's not difficult to understand why many Wiccans use Craft names. Though I didn't discuss this subject in *Wicca: A Guide for the Solitary Practitioner*, it deserves some comment here.

To cut to the heart of this matter: is it necessary for you to adopt a Wiccan name? If you wish your Wicca to correspond to conventional Wicca as far as is possible, yes. If you feel freer than these constraints, adoption of a special name isn't necessary. Once again, the decision is yours alone.

The major reason for utilizing a Craft name, as mentioned above, is that it represents the Wiccan you. For some, use of this name gives them a sense of power and mystery which they may otherwise not feel. We live in such a mundane world that it can indeed be difficult to "switch on" the magical side of our nature. Thus, use of a Wiccan name may assist in altering the conscious mind and preparing it for ritual.

Some people take an entirely different approach: they legally adopt their Wiccan name. Thus, Sally Thompson becomes Amber; Frank Jones, Greywolf. This name may even appear on driver's licenses, leases and other documents. This legal avenue is inadvisable unless you're completely open about your religion, since such a name will naturally draw attention to its bearer. Though many state that they've chosen to use their new name to the exclusion of the old one purely for spiritual reasons, most are also making a public statement regarding their religion—and not all of us are ready for such a step.

How do you find your magical name?

There are many approaches. Some Wiccans adopt the name of a Goddess or God, in honor of Them. Others look into their family's cultural history and choose a name from the associated folklore: a person with British ancestry may opt for a name culled from British folklore. Many contemporary American Wiccans incorporate an animal in their name, such as "Howling Wolf" or "Sweeping Eagle". Flower and plant names (such as Rose, Oak Keeper, Grove, Fir, Ash) are other possibilities.

You may also simply make up a name. Many Wiccan names consist of two words that have been put together. Such names are usually quite descriptive.

Some famous Wiccan names have been published. Gerald Gardner (one of the people who formed Wicca into the religion as we know it today) publicly used the name Scire. At least one of Doreen Valiente's magical names was Ameth. A well-known High Priest adopted the public Craft name of Phoenix.

Still other popular names include: Morgan, Morgana, Morgaine, Morgraine, Lugh and Arthur (all associated with Celtic mythology); Ariadne, Diana, Hermes, Poseidon, Cassandra and Triton (Greek and Roman mythology); Selket, Ma 'at, Osiris, and other Egyptian names.

(Among the most commonly used names are Amber, Phoenix and Merlin. Calling out one of these names at a Pagan gathering will usually cause many heads to turn.)

So there are plenty of possibilities from which to choose. If you decide to use a Wiccan name in ritual, always use it. Use it in prayer. Use it in rituals. Write it, in runes or in English, on your tools. You may even wish to perform some sort of name-adoption ritual. This could consist of casting a circle and invoking the Goddess and God to be present and asking Them to recognize you by your new name.

Use of a Craft name may not give you any additional power, but it's a traditional practice, and many enjoy it.

5: SELF-INITIATION

The most controversial subject matter in this book's predecessor was undoubtedly the chapter concerning initiation. Many Wiccan book reviewers were displeased with a simple idea presented within that chapter: that initiation isn't always a process that one human being performs on another. Some misinterpreted my words to the point that they believed I stated that initiation was to be avoided at all costs—a curious conclusion from my writing. (Not surprisingly, such comments were made by initiated coven members.) Some reviewers actually assumed that I'd never been initiated, and that this was the reason for my 'incorrect' views on the subject.

There are many types of initiations. Some are performed in a circle with others. Some are performed alone. Still others are never performed, but occur spontaneously within a Wiccan student's life.

An initiation into a coven (and thus into Wicca) is effective only if initiator and candidate are in perfect harmony, working within a mutually satisfactory Wiccan system or tradition. I've seen botched initiations and glorious initiations. *Any* initiation *isn't* better than no initiation, if it's performed for the wrong reasons (egotism, power over others) by the wrong person, or by the wrong coven. The rite itself isn't as important as its impact on the candidate and the spirit in which it's performed.

Though a physical initiation isn't necessary to practice Wicca, it is a ritual statement of one's allegiance to the Craft. The initiate can, from that day forward, clearly claim that they're Wiccan, for they have memories of a specific date that ceremonially began this kinship. This is important for some; for others, it's of little or no importance.

You have the right to perform a self-initiation. No one can take this right from you. If you've worked Wiccan ritual, met with the Goddess and God, have grown comfortable with Wicca, and have decided that it's your path, there's no reason on the Goddess' green Earth why you shouldn't undergo a self-initiation.

You may wish to perform a self-initiation found in a book; adapt a group initiation, or create your own. (The rite included in Chapter 12 of *Wicca* was a self-dedication—not an initiation. However, it could be incorporated into a full initiation.)

Before self-initiation, consider whether you've gained enough Wiccan experience to enter Wicca. Wiccan ritual experience is essential (reading doesn't count) before self-initiating yourself. A self-initiation rite performed by a person after, say, a year of study and ritual will be a rich and spiritually significant event, simply because the rite was preceded by the experience that makes it genuine. In other words, one can't become Wiccan (even a Solitary one) overnight.

This period of self-training and experience is absolutely vital. Yes, you'll learn the uses of the tools; the meanings of the Sabbats, the casting of the circle—but you'll also be meeting with the Goddess and the God. Becoming attuned to and establishing a relationship with Them is the heart of Wicca, and it takes time and dedication.

I'm hearing complaints.

"Sure, but during some initiations the initiator passes power to the candidate." *During a self-initiation, the Goddess and God pass power to the candidate.*

"But such initiations won't be recognized by covens." *Solitary Wiccans don't belong to covens.*

"Real initiations are designed to alter consciousness within the candidate." *So, too, are properly designed self-initiations.*

"Real initiations symbolize the death of the old (non-Wiccan) self and the rebirth of the Wiccan person." *These can be incorporated into self-initiations.*

Self-initiation is largely what you make it, but for the most satisfying results every such ritual should include the following steps. (What follows is the barest ritual outline. I've left out such things as lighting candles and charcoal.)

- Purification of some kind. (A shower or bath is fine.)

- The laying of the altar. (Use whatever tools you normally work with.)

- The circle casting. (Though this isn't absolutely necessary, it certainly heightens the atmosphere. It's best if you've already gained proficiency in circle casting before initiation. If you feel comfortable casting the circle, use it. If not, don't.)

- Opening invocations to the Goddess and the God. (These may be those that you use in your everyday Wiccan ritual work, or special ones composed for this rite

- A symbolic death of your old, non-Wiccan self. (Be creative. This may consist of wrapping yourself in black cloth; blindfolding yourself while sitting before the altar [not while walking]; even singing a dirge. Create a prayer appropriate for this moment. After a suitable time of meditation and reflection, cast off the trappings of death with a cry of joy.

- Pray anew to the Goddess and God, dedicating yourself to them. State that you're now a Wiccan. If you've chosen a magical name (see Chapter 4), saying it aloud: "I, Dione, am now a Wiccan." would be a suitable formula for inclusion in your dedicatory prayer.

- Relax in the circle for a few minutes. Watch the candle's flames. If you've brought cakes and wine into the circle, it's time to dedicate them and to share in the manifested love of the Goddess and God When you've finished your sacred meal, thank the Goddess and God for Their attendance and close the circle.

Conventional Wiccans may argue with this self-initiatory plan, but it's effective. I've presented it here as a pattern that others may use to create their own.

The Goddess and God, as the source of all life, health, food, the earth, the stars, the sun and moon and the universe, are also the true sources of initiation.

Self-initiation is an important ritual and isn't to be undergone lightly. The Wiccan should be ready for both spiritual and physical change following this rite. After all, once you've undergone a self-initiation, you're no longer just a student; you're a Wiccan: one of the few remaining humans who've decided to step past the veil of the materially-based world. You're now one of those who respects the Earth; who pours wine into sacred cups by candlelight surrounded by incense smoke; who communes with the Goddess and God in private meditation; who joyfully uses magic as a tool of positive change.

Self-initiation is a wonderful affirmation of our dedication to Wicca if it's performed for positive reasons, at the appropriate time, in the proper state of mind. If you haven't already ritually joined us, you'll know if—and when—it's time.

Initiation is no less than the beginning of a new life.

6: THE WICCAN MYSTERIES

Some readers and reviewers have complained that Wiccan books—mine included—don't contain "Wiccan mysteries." Such comments are quite true. Most books written about Wicca are either overviews of its practice or are instructions for the beginner. Wiccan writers can easily become caught up in describing circle castings, the proper use of tools, deity concepts and group dynamics. There's little room in such books for mysticism.

However, there's another reason. Mysteries are, by their very nature, difficult to frame in language. They can't truly be taught; they can only be experienced. Some manifest on other planes of existence. Many have profound emotional, psychic or spiritual effects. Some occur solely between a Wiccan and the Goddess; others between two or more Wiccans in circle.

Perhaps I'd better define my terms. First, the term 'Wiccan mysteries', as I use it here, doesn't refer to secret rituals, prayers or magical techniques, no matter how secret or effective they may be. Instead, it refers to extraordinary spiritual experiences and revelations of the highest order from the Goddess and God. The Wiccan mysteries can never be outwardly displayed. Wiccan Sabbats and Esbats celebrate them, but only in symbolic form.

If you're entirely confused at this point, it's okay. After all, these are the Wiccan *mysteries*, and this isn't the easiest topic about which to write or discuss.

One of the complaints of many Solitary Wiccans is that their rituals seem to lack depth of involvement and great spiritual meaning. There are many possible origins for this problem, but it could very well be a lack of knowledge of the Wiccan mysteries. This inner lore, when called upon in ritual, greatly enhances the proceedings.

Why? Because as previously stated, most Wiccan rituals are in some way celebrations of Wiccan mysteries. This may immediately give you a clue as to the nature of the mysteries: what are the Sabbats all about? The major, outward concept is the observation of the seasons. Once you begin to look at the seasons, you'll find a rich trove of possible Wiccan mystery material. In the mysteries, everything is both symbolic and quite real.

Most of the Wiccan mysteries relate to the Goddess and God and these have been placed within the context of sacred activities. Other mysteries are more Earth-based but, since the Goddess is the Earth, we're right back to Her.

It's possible for you to discover such mysteries. All the accumulated lore and mysteries of Wiccan traditions were discovered at some point. You can certainly continue this process to give body and depth to your Wiccan practice.

Wiccan mysteries may be discovered during meditation in ritual settings. They may be perceived while taking a walk, appear in our minds during sleep, even come in answer to fervent prayers to the Goddess and God. Such arcane secrets are usually only revealed to those who are truly involved with Wicca, for who else would have need of them?

On the other hand, some Wiccan mysteries are constantly occurring around us where we see the divine touch of the Goddess and God. However, such processes are only Wiccan mysteries once we become totally aware of them on every level of our beings.

If this is confusing, here's an example. A ripe apple falls onto the ground. It decomposes; fresh soil is blown over the fallen fruit. Rains fall. The sun heats the earth. A sprout struggles up from a seed contained within the apple. Within a few years, a new apple tree stands where the fruit had once fallen. A ripe apple falls onto the ground.

How is this a Wiccan mystery?

- These processes (fall and rise; death and rebirth, etc.) are governed by and are created by the Goddess and God, the sole sources of fertility, life and death.

- Such natural processes don't relate solely to apples; these cycles are evident in all the world.

- A Wiccan becomes aware of this process by watching the apple fall and seeing it eventually sprout. By narrowing her or his focus to this one cycle, for at least a few minutes each day, the Wiccan aligns her or his consciousness with the processes of the Goddess and God. She or he may further meditate upon this process' meaning.

- This realignment of consciousness creates a new awareness of the Goddess and God both within the world and within the self. This greater awareness creates deeper spiritual connections with Them. Additionally, the apple that served as the lesson-giver may become a powerful and profound ritual tool in this Wiccan's religious practice, symbolizing life, death and rebirth—three of the greatest mysteries that ever furrowed the human brow.

- Finally, the apple's journey may become a potent spiritual memory that immediately unlocks the silver and gold avenues to the Goddess and to the God. In this Wiccan's mind, the apple becomes more than a memory of a fruit; more than a symbol: it becomes a direct link between Them and Us; a tangible reminder of intangible things; a symbol that's not only between the worlds, but that serves as a bridge. The apple then, in this Wiccan's mysteries, may be: the Celtic cauldron of regeneration; the womb of the Goddess; a symbol of birth and rebirth; representative of the underworld and the overworld; the Earth itself, upon which so many mysteries await our discovery.

The secret of the Wiccan mysteries is that there are no secrets. You need only alter your perceptions and sharpen your focus. Look beyond the material world to the timeless processes at work within it to discover Wiccan mysteries. Or spend time in ritual meditation specifically to deepen your understanding of the subtlest aspects of Wicca, the Goddess and the God.

Then, after you've discovered them, you can celebrate and sing and dance in circles created of light and love and re-experience these mysteries time and again. Rituals may be enlarged to include recognition of such experiences, or special rites may be performed in their honor.

The point here is that true Wiccan mysteries can't be found within Books of Shadows or in ancient secrets or within the words of others. They can only be found within our relationship with the Goddess and God, and in our understanding of nature as an illustration of Their energy.

Want some more hints?

Watch a birth.

Watch the sun melting ice.

Watch the unfurling of leaves on trees in the spring.

Watch the ocean.

Watch the clouds drifting far above.

Watch rain splattering onto pools of water.

Watch lightning crackling and sparking against the night sky.

Watch smoke rising from a sacred bonfire.

Watch an eclipse.

Watch a cat hunting in the backyard.

Watch a baby rediscovering our world.

✪   ✪   ✪

Don't only watch these things; experience them. Feel them. Then you'll have begun to draw the Wiccan mysteries closer to you. You'll have the rare opportunity to fleetingly draw back the veil that we've thrown over our world and see the face of the Goddess....

And the Wiccan mysteries will be yours.

7: EVERYDAY WICCA

I've already stated that, ideally, religion permeates all aspects of life. Even when we're not lighting candles and casting circles, it's best to live in a Wiccan manner. Life itself can be seen as a ritual to the Goddess and God.

Many, however, have difficulty in finding the spiritual nature of their everyday lives. We can become mesmerized by the smoke and mirrors of society's trappings and diversions; equally, our home life, employment, bills and other mundane factors can weigh us down until we begin to question whether we ever spiritually felt a thing.

The solution isn't more ritual; it consists of subtly shifting our focus from solely physical forces and objects to the inherently spiritual nature of everything. Washing dishes can become an exploration of the powers of the element of Water. Working is an opportunity to feel the energy of other people. Cleaning up the yard teaches us important lessons regarding the seasons. Even attending school is an exercise in utilizing (and, hopefully, expanding) our consciousness, and viewing the lessons from a spiritual standpoint can be quite enlightening.

Indeed, a Wiccan viewpoint can get us through hard times, just as can adherence to any other religion. To be able to tap this source of peace, however, we must first realize that Wicca isn't limited to ritual, prayer and magic. Wicca is a way of life as much as it's a religion.

Applying Wicca's principles to our world is one of the simplest methods of bringing Wicca into our daily lives. The following discussions are suggestions. You may have different interpretations.

Harm none. Think about this when someone cuts you off on the road; steals 'your' parking space; is rude to you, or when you're facing all manner of trouble with mates, family, neighbors, friends or co-workers. Remembering this code allows us to rise above anger, jealousy and hatred, and may even transform such potentially destructive emotions into positive energies. It also presents the opportunity to care for ourselves by reducing stress. (I'll be the first to admit that this is far from easy.)

Reincarnation reminds us that we have more than one chance at life. This concept negates suicide as a solution to problems, or as an easy way out, since we'll be back sooner or later to confront those same issues that we believed were too difficult to face in this life. Additionally, thoughts of reincarnation can help us through periods of mourning. It can also free us of fear of death.

Karma. This concept states that right action is returned with positive energy, and negative action is returned with negativity. It's allied with 'harm none' and is again a quick reminder to act in a positive fashion. Additionally, we can see how good (positive; beneficial) actions are in themselves acts of spirituality.

Some Wiccans express a slightly different concept known as the law of three or the threefold law. This states that anything we do returns to us in triple strength. Thus, a small act of caring may be returned to us as a great act of caring by someone else. A petty act of revenge may result in great harm against us. The law of three is simply a different understanding of karma.

Magic reminds us that we do, indeed, have control over our lives. If we don't like them, we can change them through positive ritual. However, magic also teaches us patience: a cauldron placed on an open fire never immediately comes to a boil, and magic doesn't immediately manifest. We may also be able to see little bits of magic at work in our everyday lives—and this can be comforting.

Thought teaches us that thoughts are things; that is, thoughts generate and release energy and, if repeated with intent, can be powerful sources of energy. Thus, as we control negative thoughts, we improve our lives. Simply refusing to recognize a negative thought and changing our focus from the negative ("I have no money") to the positive ("I've got enough food to eat") can produce dramatic effects. And so, because we can improve our lives and harm none by positive thinking, even our throughts can be expressions of spirituality.

Earth stewardship (caring for our planet) is another of Wicca's most important concepts. There's nothing particularly spiritual about filling a garbage can or chopping down a tree—two actions that are in violation of Wiccan principles.

However, rinsing and reusing bottles; recycling paper, aluminum cans, plastic and glass *is* an act of spirituality, for we're caring for our planet. Similarly, planting a tree; tending gardens; giving gifts of plants to others; refusing to use artificial pesticides; donating to ecological causes; writing letters in support of preserving endangered animals and their environments (forests, wetlands and other environmentally sensitive areas) are all further expressions of Wicca's concern and love for our planet. Even political involvement, when it truly leads to better Earth stewardship, can have its rewarding spiritual aspects.

The continuous presence of the Goddess and God is another important Wiccan teaching. If we're on the Earth, we're with the Goddess and God. No part of us or our lives is divorced from Them, unless we deem that this is true. In the heart of roaring cities; in the quiet of a country valley; in a mobile home roasting in the desert, the Goddess and God are there. In our office, school, neighborhood and favorite store, the Goddess and God are there. In rush-hour traffic; in long lines at the bank; in the flowers and plants on our window sills, the Goddess and God are there.

The omnipresence of our deities isn't some exalted spiritual sentiment; it's true. The Earth isn't represented by the Goddess; it is a part of Her. She is everywhere. Similarly, She is also within us, as is the God. Thus, whatever we do, wherever we go, from a convenience store to a concert in the park, They are present. Remembering this fact may, once again, reveal the inherent spirituality in many situations.

OTHER METHODS OF ENHANCING EVERYDAY SPIRITUALITY

Make an offering to the Goddess and God each day (see Chapter 10: offerings, prayers, etc.).

Set aside at least five minutes a day as "sacred time". During this five minutes you can simply think about your place in life and Wicca's role, or you can perform other activities directly or indirectly related to Wicca. (Once again, reading can't be considered as sacred time.) Here are some examples of what you might do:

Morning and evening meditations

Working arts or crafts with a Wiccan theme

Listening to classical or contemporary Pagan music

Tending or planting plants

Volunteering

Recycling

Journalizing (writing) about your Wiccan involvement

Corresponding with other Wiccans

Meditating (or psychically attuning) with stones

Writing new rituals

Experimenting with new methods of divination

Collecting magical herbs

Visiting gardens or parks

Listening and communicating with animals

Reading Pagan fairy tales (there really isn't any other
    kind) to your children

This list can be greatly extended. Indeed, once we begin to think of how Wicca has influenced our lives, a wide range of activities can be performed during such sacred time.

This chapter has been a short introduction to some methods of strengthening the Wiccan nature of your life. In this pursuit, action is as important as thought.

Blessed Be.

PART TWO:

PRACTICE

8: EFFECTIVE PRAYER

Prayer is little-discussed in Wiccan books, probably because it is, by its very nature, a highly personal experience. Additionally, most Wiccan books seem to be more concerned with describing ritual motivations and mechanics than with delving into the truly spiritual aspects of our religion.

But behind the circles, the altars and the regalia, Wicca is designed to facilitate contact with the divine. We can certainly contact Them during our rites with memorized invocations, but what of non-ritual occasions? Will They hear us? Will they speak to us?

Of course. In Wicca, ritual is a framework in which prayer and magic take place. But prayer isn't solely a ritualistic act. We can pray at any time, and, utilizing our connections with the Goddess and God, contact Them for assistance and comfort.

Following are discussions of some aspects of Wiccan prayer.

PRAYER IS DIRECTED BOTH
WITHIN AS WELL AS WITHOUT

Many religions preach that our bodies are filthy, disgusting things that even their deities dislike and hate. Such faiths deny the flesh and turn their eyes toward the skies when seeking the divine.

Most Wiccans, however, accept that the Goddess and God are within ourselves as well as outside us. If everything in nature is connected through subtle but real energies, so too are we linked with the Goddess and God.

We must become more intimately familiar with this connection. We can't accomplish this by searching our bodies and asking, "Where's the Goddess? Where's the God?" They don't reside in any one part of us; They're simply within. They exist within our DNA. They're present in our souls. The Goddess and God are infused into every aspect of our beings.

We gain familiarity with the divine spark within ourselves through ritual, meditation and prayer. It's during these moments, in which we expand our awareness beyond the physical world, that the divine energy within us rises and fills our consciousness. Though we may call the Goddess and God, we're actually becoming newly focused on Their presence inside us. Once this has occurred, we can become aware of Their greater presences beyond ourselves.

Prayer is the process of attuning and communicating with the Goddess and God. During prayer, we may call Them from the Moon, the Sun and the stars, from the seas, the deserts and caves, from the haunts of wild animals; from the Earth itself: but the call must first move us, must first renew our awareness of the Goddess and God within, before it can contact the universally manifested deities.

We might see a bunch of ripe peaches hanging from a tree and feel great desire to eat one. However, until we narrow our focus on just one peach, approach it and pluck it from the tree, we won't satisfy our craving. In prayer, we must narrow our focus, at first, upon the Goddess and God within, before we can contact the greater understanding of the Goddess and God.

This initial focus may be accomplished through words, visualizations, songs or by other means. There are no governing rules, though I present a few suggestions below. Experiment to discover the most effective technique.

To begin, a Wiccan adopts a prayerful attitude (see below). She may then begin each prayer with the following words:

O Goddess Within,

O God Within,

While saying these words, she shifts her consciousness to the warm, peaceful memories of her previous contacts with Them. This may put her into the proper mode of consciousness. She could then proceed to say:

O Goddess of the Moon, Waters and Earth;

O God of the Forests and Mountains;

This expands her conception of the Goddess and God, and contacts a greater part of Them. Once she's achieved a stronger connection, she then speaks to Them in specifics (i.e., states the reason for her prayer).

Wiccan prayer, then, isn't addressed to some distant deities who reside in alien cloud palaces. We needn't use a bullhorn to call to the Goddess and God. Rather, we need only become newly aware of Them within us. This is the secret.

PRAYERFUL ATTITUDES

Many people, of all religious persuasions, pray only in times of great need, terrific stress or spiritual crisis. This is a part of human nature: when all else fails, appeal to higher forces. Prayers at such times are certainly appropriate, and can often provide just what we need to get through such periods. However, they're not the ideal prayerful occasions, for we often don't take the time to truly contact the Goddess and God before we begin our communication. This may block the prayer's effectiveness.

Thus, it's quite important, even in moments of extreme desperation, to adopt a prayerful attitude before speaking to the Goddess and God. A prayerful attitude consists of peace and hope resting on an unshakable spiritual foundation.

It may be quite difficult to adopt such a state when a friend has just become ill, a child has run away from home, your cat is missing. However, attaining this peaceful, hopeful, spiritual state will lend greater power to your prayer, for it will allow you to more directly connect with the Goddess and God. Once you've linked with the Goddess and God, you can be as emotional as you wish.

Urgent, wild prayers ("Goddess, help me!") or demanding prayers ("You gotta help me out. Right now!") will lend you little or no spiritual support, and probably won't go farther than your lips or mind. A few of these prayers may indeed reach the Goddess and God, if their speaker is sufficiently aware of her or his connection with Them. However, they're far from the most effective form of prayer.

Such prayers are usually spontaneous. They may be the product of new information or fresh insight into a situation. Thus, they certainly can't be planned in advance. Or can they?

Indeed they can be. With a bit of practice and thought, you can transform ineffective prayers to quite effective prayers. How? Simply pray every day, in a prayerful attitude. Talk to the Goddess and God about positive events in your life. Thank Them for manifested prayers. Speak to Them about the moonrise, the sound of the birds in the morning, the new kittens. Speak to Them, too, of your needs and hopes and desires.

Make prayer a daily occurrence. Don't wait to pray solely during those rare occasions when crushing need forces you to turn to Them for assistance. Prayer – true prayer – on a daily basis sets up a regular line of communication. So long as you don't recite prayers without emotion or feeling, this prayer experience will come in handy when you're faced with a crisis. Your prayer may still be quick and to the point, but you'll have established a firm line of communication and have the capability to use it at any time.

Prayer should always be respectful. Wiccans don't bargain with the Goddess and God. We don't say, "Okay, Goddess. Give me that new car and I'll burn a candle for you for three full moons." That's not Wiccan. We never bargain with the Goddess and God. Prayer doesn't consist of deal-making.

We also never threaten or order around the Goddess and God in prayer. Doing so reveals that we've attempted to elevate ourselves to Goddess- and God-hood. Sorry; we're not deities.

Few people enjoy being commanded; no goddesses or gods enjoy it. Such 'prayers' have no place in Wicca. (This statement doesn't mean that it only has no place in my form of Wicca; it's universal. It isn't dependent upon your personal conception of the Goddess and God; it's dependent upon the nature of things: the Goddess and God are bigger than us. End of discussion.)

And so, having a prayerful attitude means being in a peaceful, hopeful, spiritual state. If you attain this prior to praying, your prayers will be that much more effective.

THE NATURE OF PRAYER

Many religious people will argue that prayer consists only of communication between humans and the divine. As Wiccans, however, we're aware of the non-physical energies contained within our bodies (the same energies used in creating the circle, in consecrating tools and in other works of magic). Effective prayer consists of more than words, for when prayers are made in the correct state, with pure, unadulterated emotion, we release energy with our words and direct it to the Goddess and God. Thus, certain forms of prayer (those in which we make requests, for example) are also acts of magic.

We needn't attempt to make true prayer into a magical act; (that is, we don't have to arouse, program and direct energy during prayer); this automatically occurs during emotional prayer. Fixing our minds upon a need, contacting the Goddess and God, and speaking to Them stirs up, programs and directs energy. It is an act of magic.

If we're not properly attuned with the Goddess and God – if we're not clearly focused – the energy raised by the prayer flies off into outer space in a willy-nilly fashion to no effect. Just as we must gather droplets of water into a tub to take a bath, so too must we gather our energies and direct them to the Goddess and God. To do otherwise is to perform ineffective prayer. Therefore, we must maintain our focus on Them and allow nothing to distract us.

Don't misunderstand this. Though some types of prayer can be considered to be spells, this certainly isn't true of all forms. Additionally, praying to the Goddess and God isn't spell casting; it's a religious act that happens to have a magical content.

Wiccan prayer is far more than a simple recitation of facts to the Goddess and God and more than form of communication. It's a flow of personal energy from a human to the deities.

TYPES OF PRAYERS

There are many types of prayers: prayers of thanks, of celebration, of need. Situations obviously frame the nature of most prayers. However, praying only when in need is using the least of prayer's potential. The following prayers are merely examples.

Prayers of thanks are just that:

O Goddess within;

O God within;

O Goddess of the Moon, Waters and Earth;

O God of the Forests and Mountains:

I give thanks for _____ (or, for my many blessings).

The prayer may then continue on to describe how this blessing has changed her or his life:

Thank you for lending me spiritual strength in this time of need; it has refreshed and encouraged me.

Or:

Thank you for assisting me in finding the perfect home; we're safe now.

Or:

Thank you for touching my life and allowing me to find Mr. (or Ms.) Right; my world is filled with love and happiness.

Such prayers may be quite lengthy. In prayers of thanks, it's best to detail your specific reasons for thankfulness. This strengthens the fact that the Goddess and God have recently assisted you, and also strengthens the prayer's effectiveness.

If you need assistance in creating a ritual, you may pray for this:

O Glorious Goddess;

O Gracious God;

You who created all that is;

Help me create this ritual

In Your honor

At the time of the full moon (or Yule and so on).

Prayers of celebration may also be framed when the Wiccan has accomplished a tremendous feat, with or without the direct assistance of the Goddess and God:

O Gracious Goddess,

I passed the test.

Or:

O Mother Goddess

O Father God

I finished (the book, the song, the garden).

Prayers of need are just that:

O Goddess within;

O God within;

O Goddess of the Moon, the Waters, and the Earth,

O God of the Forests and Mountains;

O Shining Ones of Infinite Wisdom:

Teach me to understand my child (friend, lover, parents, boss).

Lend me the spiritual strength to overcome my anger and pain;

Quench my fires with love.

Certainly, there are many types of need. In our market economy, where we must work to earn money to buy things that others create, our needs are often physical: we need a new car, a home, a good job, more money. Prayers of need may also be involved with healing, compassion, love, protection and many other aspects of daily human life.

At times, our needs may seem insurmountable. We may temporarily lose our Goddess and God focus and descend into negative thinking, disillusionment and fear.

It's at such times that we may pray to them:

O Goddess within;

O God within;

O Goddess of the Moon, the Waters and the Earth;

O God of the Forests and Mountains:

I need to feel Your presence.

I need to be reminded of You.

Assist me to remember Your lessons;

Show me the key that will unlock my spirituality.

Blessed Be.

Or, we may pray regarding problems that we're having with our religion: After the introductory part of the prayer, you may say:

> *Goddess, I simply don't understand this. This book says that we never incarnate as the opposite sex of the one that we are in this life. Help.*

Or,

> *Goddess and God, I'm trying to find the perfect circle casting. Guide my mind, heart and hands as I try to figure this out.*

Keep in mind that, to be effective, all prayers of need must be stated with a prayerful attitude.

Wiccan prayer is a private, personal aspect of our religion. We all have our own methods of contacting the Goddess and God. However, the techniques outlined in this chapter may be of assistance in truly contacting Them, and of using prayer as a positive, supportive tool of everyday life.

Pray often – it's an essential part of Wicca.

9: DAILY PRAYER AND CHANTS

Our religion reveres the Goddess and God. As such, it's vital that we establish and maintain our relationships with Them. Everyday life presents many opportunities to strengthen this bond. Short prayers when we rise in the morning, before meals, before sleep and at other times of the day are highly appropriate.

This chapter includes a variety of both simple and formal prayers for many occasions. Feel free to use them as is or as a guide for creating your own. Though I've generically addressed these to the Goddess and God, you can use the names by which you've grown to know Them.

Daily prayer, both formal and spontaneous, is another method of truly making Wicca a part of your everyday life. The exact words don't matter much, for it's your involvement in the prayer that's most important.

EVERYDAY PRAYERS AND CHANTS

A Prayer Before Meals

Before eating, say these or similar words (if necessary, whisper or merely think these words):

From forest and stream;

From mountain and field;

From the fertile Earth's

Nourishing yield;

I now partake of
Divine energy;
May it lend health,
Strength and love to me.
Blessed Be.

Another Prayer Before Meals

Goddess of the verdant plain;
God of sun-ripe grain;
Goddess of the cooling rain;
God of fruit and cane;
Bless this meal I've prepared;
Nourish me with love;
Bless this meal I now share
With You both above.

A Third Prayer Before Meals

O Goddess within,
O God within,
I now partake of the
Fertility of the Earth.
Bless this food with Your love.

A Morning Prayer

Bless this day, sun of fiery light.
Bless this day; prepare me for the night.

Sunrise Chant

> *Fire growing,*
> *Sun is glowing;*
> *Glowing, flowing*
> *Down on me.*

Another Morning Prayer

> *0 Gracious Goddess,*
> *0 Gracious God,*
> *Lend me health, strength and love*
> *During this coming day.*
> *Assist me with the challenges ahead.*
> *Share Your divine wisdom.*
> *Teach me to respect all things.*
> *Remind me that the greatest power of all is love.*
> *Blessed Be.*

An Evening Prayer

> *The moon illuminates the earth*
> *With wondrous silver rays;*
> *Illuminate me through the night*
> *And through the sun-lit days.*

A Prayer Before Sleep

> *0 Gracious Goddess;*
> *0 Gracious God,*
> *I now enter the realm of dreams.*

Weave now, if You will, a web of protective light around me.
Guard both my sleeping form and my spirit.
Watch over me
Until the sun once again
Rules the Earth.
0 Gracious Goddess,
0 Gracious God,
Be with me through the night.

Invocation Before Sleep

Lady of the Moon;
Lord of the Sun;
Protect me and mine
Now day is done.

New Moon Chant

Silver flowing,
Diana's growing;
Growing, showing
Love for me.

A Short Chant For Help

Divine Mother,
Mother Divine,
Show me the way;
Give me a sign.

10: PRAYERS AND RITES OF THANKS AND OFFERINGS

OFFERING RITES

Many Wiccans follow ancient custom by making a small offering to the Goddess and God on a daily basis. This is usually done before images of deities, but may also be performed anywhere, including outside.

Making consistent offerings to the Goddess and God reinforces your involvement with both Them and our religion, so there's every reason to make periodic offerings.

The main tool of such rites is the offertory bowl, into which the offering is placed (if indoors). Though this may be of any natural material, a clay, wooden, ceramic or silver bowl is preferred.

What type of offerings are best? Generally, food in any form (save for meat) is fine, as are all small, precious objects. Even jewelry and expensive items are sometimes offered and buried in the Earth. If you have nothing else, and can spare no food, pure water (which is not only necessary to human life but is also filled with Goddess energy) can be used. Incense may also be smoldered in offering, but it should be a special type that you don't ordinarily burn. (I wish that it wasn't necessary for me to say so, but just in case some of you have missed an important lesson: we never sacrifice living things to the deities.)

Offerings must be consciously made, done with thanks, intent and focus. Empty offerings will have little effect. In past times, such offerings were considered vital to the worshipper's continuing existence. Today, we might see them as vital to our spiritual existence.

You may decide to make an offering once a day, once a week or once a month, every three weeks, every full moon. (Rhythms of this type are preferred rather than haphazard offerings) The time of day isn't really important, though most prefer the night. Again: find your own best plan.

Offerings certainly can also be made at any time in thanks for answered prayer.

The rites that follow are suggestions. Use your intuition and experiment to find the forms best suited to you.

After making the offering, reflect for a few moments on the meaning of your actions.

A Daily Offering

Place the offering in the bowl (or in the ground) while saying:

What I take I freely give.

Accept this offering, Goddess and God.

Another Daily Offering

Make the offering while saying;

I give you this symbol of my devotion.

May it strengthen my bonds with you.

An Offering for a Special Request

This should by no means be seen as a bribe. We don't bribe the Goddess and God, for They created and possess everything in existence. However, giving an offering before making a special request (during prayer) is again a symbol of our need. The actual energy that exists within the offering is sent by the power of our prayer to the Goddess and God, and so further emphasizes our need.

When you have a special request, choose a suitable offering: something quite important to you, either emotionally, mentally or monetarily. Bury it in the Earth while praying for the request.

It is done.

(Never dig up and retrieve offerings. Once you've given them to the Goddess and God, you've relinquished their physical forms. What's done is done.)

RITES OF THANKS

Thanks for An Answered Prayer

Goddess

What no human ear could hear, you heard.

What no human eye could see, you saw.

What no human heart could bear, you transformed.

What no human hand could do, you did.

What no human power could change, you changed.

Goddess of love; Goddess omnipotent;

You through Whom all power flows;

Source of all;

Queen of the Cosmos;

Creatrix of the Universe;

Accept this humble token of thanks

From a Solitary Wiccan

Who has spoken

And who has been heard.

(Place an offering, such as a flower, a coin, a jewel, a picture that you've drawn, or some other object precious to you on the earth. Or, bury it in the earth. If this can't be immediately done, place the object in the offering bowl and later give it directly to the Earth.)

A Solitary Ritual of Thanks

(You alone will know when to perform this ritual. It can be done at any phase of the moon, during the day or night, whenever needed.)

You'll need one large white or pink bowl; one white candle; water; small, fresh flowers (white blooms are best) and one piece of white cotton cloth.

Place the bowl on the altar (or on any table). If desired, cast a circle. Affix the white candle to the center of the bowl with warmed beeswax or with drippings from another white candle (so that the bowl acts as a candle holder).

Pour water into the bowl. Float the fresh flowers on the surface of the water. Light the candle.

Visualize your reason for the ritual; remember why you're thanking the Goddess and God. Touch the water on both sides of the candle with your fingertips, saying these or similar words:

Lady of the Moon, of the stars and the Earth;

Lord of the Sun, of the forests and the hills;

I perform a ritual of thanks.

My love shines like the flame;

My love floats like the petals

Upon You.

Lady of the Waters, of flowers and the sea;

Lord of the Air, of horns and of fire;

I perform a ritual of thanks.
My love shines like the flame;
My love floats like the petals
Upon You.
Lady of the Caves, of cats and snakes;
Lord of the Plains, of falcons and stags;
I perform a ritual of thanks.
My love shines like the flame;
My love floats like the petals
Upon You.

Look into the candle's flame, then down into the water. Blow gently upon the water's surface and watch the flower's movements. Meditate. Commune. Thank.

When it's time, remove the petals from the water. Place them in the center of the white cotton cloth. Wrap the cloth around the petals. If you've cast a circle, close it now. End your rite of thanks by quenching the candle's flame, pouring the water onto the ground and burying the flowers in the Earth. It is done.

11: SIMPLE WICCAN RITES

You're excited about an upcoming trip. Then you realize that your travel plans will interfere with the celebration of a Sabbat or Esbat. Since it wouldn't be practical (or advisable) to take along all your ritual tools, what can you do?

On other occasions, the desire or need for a ritual may suddenly occur. When this occurs there's little or no time for preparation. You may hear that a friend is in the hospital; that someone you love is in danger. Again, what are the options?

The answer lies in simplified Wiccan rites. In certain circumstances, a magical working (such as folk magic) may be more appropriate. For strictly spiritual occasions, even less complex rituals can produce powerful changes of consciousness and satisfying connection with the Goddess and God.

Ritual tools (athame, wand, cup, censer, incense, water and salt) are assistants to ritual. They aren't necessary, but when we're beginning to learn Wicca they're of invaluable help in creating ritual consciousness, defining and purifying sacred space, and invoking the Goddess and God. Once we've mastered the basics, such tools are always welcomed, but aren't necessary. Simplified ritual consists, as you might have guessed, of rites performed with a minimum of tools and ritual movements.

I've performed rituals with a paper packet of salt (such as is provided in some restaurants), a small paper cup of water, a birthday cake candle and a regular table knife. With the salt and water I consecrated the general area.

I used the knife to cast a small circle, and lit the candle to the Goddess and God. This was a satisfactory rite, though I'd had no ritual bath, few tools and little time to prepare.

Once, a few friends and I did an extremely simplified healing rite in a hospital room for a sick friend. I've chanted in the stillness of alien hotel rooms far from home and performed simple moon rites when I happened to see the moon peeking through the trees.

Then too, I've performed ritual with only the tools of nature, whether I was indoors or out. The earth beneath me; the water gushing before me; the air and the fiery force of the sun above. I've most often relied solely on my mind, emotions and magical visualization abilities to perform simplified Wiccan rituals.

I began practicing Wicca when I was still underage and living at home. This forced me to use simplified rituals: lighting candles and softly chanting; staring into the fire on the Sabbats; whispering full moon incantations while sitting on the window sill as I gazed up at the lunar globe.

Simply put, though the ritual tools and forms of Wicca are important because they, in part, define our religion, they're not necessary. Effective ritual isn't dependent upon the number of tools that you can pile onto the altar; it begins within you and continues from there. The tools and memorized chants are outward expressions of inward changes (such as the shift to ritual consciousness). They can assist us in creating these inner transformations, but they aren't prerequisite.

Below I present the suggested steps of all extemporaneous or greatly simplified Wiccan rites. Consider this as a pattern after which you can develop your own. The need for such rites may arise at any time, usually when you're away from home and books aren't available. To be prepared for such emergencies, think in advance of some ways in which you can perform simple yet effective Wiccan rituals at any time, and at any place, with few tools.

The following information is suitable for use during both emergency situations as well as when away from home (and tools) on the Sabbats and Esbats.

CASTING A CIRCLE

Stand, sit or lie, according to the situation. Raise energy by tightening your muscles. Visualize it glowing as a ball of purplish-blue flame within you. Using your protective hand, direct this energy out from you into a small magic circle. (The hand acts as the energy director). Alternately, send out the energy in a clockwise circle around you without moving your hand. Feel the circle shimmering and pulsing. (If desired and possible, sprinkle salt and/or water around you to bless the area before creating the circle.)

INVOKING THE GODDESS AND GOD

Prayers that you've memorized may feel right. Simply say what you feel. Remember to focus on your connections with Them while praying. If circumstances don't permit you to speak out loud, *think* your words. You might use something like this formula:

Mother Goddess, be here with me.

Father God, be here with me.

Then explain the situation or say words in celebration of the ritual occasion. These don't have to be lengthy. Here's a suggested format:

○ State the reason for the rite: recognition of a Sabbat (if so, which one), full moon, or a special need.

- State something about the occasion or ask for Their assistance, if appropriate.

- Thank the Goddess and God for their attentions. An example of this for, say, Yule might be something like this:

I come before you tonight (or today) to celebrate Yule. The sun is reborn of the Goddess.

Light is growing. The promise of spring has begun.

Meditate upon the meaning of the occasion for a few moments, then say:

Goddess and God, thank you for attending my simple circle. Hail and farewell.

You may also wish to recite memorized invocations, or say many more words. Follow your intuition.

CLOSING THE RITE

After thanking the Goddess and God, take up the energy with which you created the circle. If at all possible, eat something directly following the circle (if nothing else, taste a bit of salt). Your simplified rite has ended.

If you whisper and internalize your actions, such rituals can be performed in crowded rooms, in the presence of others, without their knowledge. You can truthfully state that you wish to pray for a few moments and in no way reveal to whom you're praying.

There's no reason to miss ritual just because you're physically distant from your tools, or have had no warning. This is one of the great advantages of Solitary Wicca: you don't have to call up the other members for ritual, nor do you have to feel that you simply can't do a ritual by yourself. You can – by using simplified Wiccan ritual.

12: MAGIC AND THE SOLITARY WICCAN

Magic is a tremendously powerful tool. With it, we can facilitate changes in both our spirituality and our physical lives. This natural (though little-understood) process of moving energy with purpose is certainly an important part of Wicca, for we (of course) create the circle in which we work our rites with magic. We may also use magic to purify and to consecrate ritual tools and jewelry.

This chapter is limited to discussions of Wiccan magic as opposed to folk magic (the non-religious use of tools such as candles, herbs, oils and colors, combined with personal power, to affect changes.)

THE CIRCLE

You should already know how to create a magic circle (or 'create sacred space') You raise energy, give it purpose and, using your mind and perhaps a tool, direct this energy outward from your body in the shape of a large sphere, in which you perform your rituals.

That much should be clear from your readings. Now, how *well* do you know this process? Do you take it for granted? Do you really know what's going on? Do you ever test the circle's strength? Have you ever felt the boundaries of the circle with an outstretched, sensitized hand? Is your circle (actually, a half-sphere) perfect? Lop-sided? Sunken? Oval-shaped? Too big?

Such questions can be answered by careful study of the next circle that you create. Using all your senses (especially your psychic abilities), examine your circle after finishing it. Give it a white glove test. Answer the questions mentioned above, then determine whether you feel different within the circle's boundaries. That's one of the clues. If you do find problems, close the circle and begin again with more attention to what you're doing.

We must never become sloppy in our circle constructions. Creating the circle is similar to building a cathedral or raising the megaliths of Stonehenge: we're building a temple, *our* temple, in which we'll worship our deities. It deserves every bit of our time, energy and attention.

RAISING ENERGY IN THE CIRCLE

This form of magic should also be familiar. A need is visualized. While visualizing, the Wiccan raises energy from within her or his body and, through the visualization, imprints this need onto the energy. The power is then released.

Unfortunately, Solitary Wiccans have few energy-raising methods available to them. The first: you're sitting before the altar. You begin to slowly chant a statement of purpose, such as 'heal her' or 'protect me'. You slowly increase the speed of the chant, never wavering in your visualization. You begin tightening the muscles all over your body (this raises physical energy, even when you're still). The power builds within you and threatens to spill over. You release it.

Another method is far more physical. You begin a slow clockwise dance (or walk) around the altar while visualizing and/or chanting the need. The dance increases in speed. When you release the power, you may fall dramatically to the floor.

Yet a third method utilizes breathing techniques which tighten the muscles and raise energy.

And that, fellow Solitaries, is just about it. There are a few other methods, but they require the presence of several other persons and are, thus, limited to covens.

SENDING THE ENERGY

In coven magical workings, power is raised by any one of a number of methods. This continues for some time until the power that's been raised reaches its peak. At this point the participants let go of the power; they may drop to the floor, completely relaxing their muscles, while pushing out the power. Those present and participating in this process can, for our purposes, be termed Energy Raisers.

Usually, but not always, this power is then directed and released through the circle by a single person – often the High Priestess. (Sometimes the energy is sent into a physical object within the circle itself.) This person, whom I'll here call the Energy sender, has the ability to take all this energy within herself and direct it outward toward its goal. (Some covens work differently. Each member may send out her or his energy. Still, the Sender is there to direct any stray energies and to control the energy-raising process that proceeds this release.)

As Solitary Wiccans, we must always be both the Energy Raiser and the Energy Sender. This demands practice and control.

The method used by coven members to release energy mentioned above is the one that we use. When it's time, simply push it out. Relax your muscles – all at once. With visualization, direct the energy outward from your hand or athame.

Some find this difficult at first. The Wiccan may feel the energy, and attempt to send it out, but may question whether it reaches its goal. Many new Solitary Wiccans also wonder how the energy penetrates the circle and actually exits, when one of the circle's functions is to retain precisely this energy.

The perfect ability to raise and send energy is one of the challenges of solitary Wicca, and will come with time. When you've properly cast a circle, you've sent energy from your body for a specific purpose, and that purpose has been achieved. Thus, you've performed a magical working.

Once you've achieved this, the next step is to raise more energy (through one of the techniques mentioned above) and then to send it a bit further, through the circle and out toward its goal.

Don't worry about the circle somehow blocking the exit of the energy. It's somewhat akin to a door. You're inside the structure, and sending energy through it opens the door. Like doors, circles don't need their functions explained to them during magic. The circle 'knows' that one of its functions is to release energy. (The door automatically shuts once the energy has left.)

Okay, you might be saying, so the circle is like a room in which we stand, and we can send energy out from it. Fine. But why doesn't the energy leak out before we're ready to send it? Because we haven't sent enough energy to open the door. Simply grasping a door knob won't cause it to open. We must exert force and pressure in the correct combination to remove the obstacle. This is true of magic as well: only a concentrated, directed stream of energy is strong enough to punch a temporary hole in the circle and travel outside its boundaries.

A coven can raise energy over an extended period of time, certainly up to half an hour or longer, through ring dances, chanting and other techniques. During this time, the coveners will of necessity release some of their energy prior to the let-it-all-out moment which is determined by the High Priestess. The circle retains this energy until such time as the combined force of all the coveners, directed by the High Priestess, opens the door.

Solitary Wiccans also raise power within the circle. And yes, we may release a bit of energy too early. Still, it's important that we hold in the energy until the last possible moment. A single energy release is most effective.

Push the energy out of you. Feel it exploding away in a focused beam of energy, shooting from you, through the circle, and out to its goal. Visualize and feel any excess energy lying around the circle as joining the main stream of energy.

Since you don't have a second person directing the energy, you must do this yourself. Fortunately, with practice, it's really quite simple. Visualize!

After every Wiccan rite, especially those that have involved magic, some energy will naturally be retained within the circle. This energy can be subtly distracting so it's usual to earth it by consuming food after each ritual. Protein foods (such as beans and corn, dairy products, and so on) are ideal. Eating shifts the consciousness back to this reality, and also replenishes some of the energy lost during magic.

These, then, have been some specifics of Solitary Wiccan magical workings. At one time they were closely-held secrets. Today, all can share in this knowledge and utilize it to improve the quality of their lives.

A few further words are perhaps appropriate. Wiccan magic must, by its performance within a circle, be for positive change. Negative magic has no place in Wicca, and doing such a working within a magic circle may immediately backfire upon the perpetrator.

Energy raised within sacred space (the circle) is directly attuned to the Goddess and God. Send Them negative energy and you're likely to instantaneously receive it back – threefold.

Over the years, many well-meaning Wiccans have warned of the 'danger' of Solitary Wicca. They've argued that a coven can act as a safety valve, defusing a covener in a volatile state of mind who wants the coven to perform a negative magical working. (No covens would perform truly negative magic.)

This argument, which on the surface seems quite satisfactory, doesn't hold water. A moral person is a moral person. Anyone who accepts the primary tenet of Wicca (harm none) won't be tempted to perform a negative magical working, whether they're a coven member or a Solitary.

It can't be stated too often – harming none means harming *none*, in any way, including yourself. ('Harming' should be thought of as interference with or the manipulation of the lives of others, and includes hexing, cursing and person-specific love spells.) Once this tenet has been accepted, and it should be by all who profess to be Wiccans, the imaginary dangers of Solitary Wiccan magic vanish.

PART THREE:

YOUR OWN
TRADITION

13: CREATING A NEW PATH

Much of conventional Wicca is organized into traditions. Since traditions, by definition, are beliefs and practices that are passed from one generation or group to another, a Wiccan tradition is a specific form of Wiccan practice that is passed to other persons, usually following initiation.

Wiccan traditions are one of our religion's strongest survival mechanisms. Structure is necessary for every religion's survival. Without it, it will crumble in confusion and chaos.

If every Wiccan constantly reinvented every aspect of Wicca (tools, ritual forms, deity concepts), our religion as we know it would soon disappear. Lacking traditional forms and beliefs, it could hardly be passed on to others.

As Solitary Wiccans, we generally don't practice a specific Wiccan tradition (unless we've been so trained and have left a coven). This presents us with great freedom. Some Solitary Wiccans create new rituals for each Sabbat and Esbat and practice a rather loose form of Wicca.

However, many Solitaries feel the need to create their own traditions so that their religious practices and beliefs are supported by a solid foundation. Though such new traditions will evolve with time and experience, they do provide a valuable framework for the Solitary Wiccan's practices. If nothing else, it provides a firm rock to grasp in the often stormy sea of self-directed worship, and is a reassurance that the Wiccan is walking the right path. In a sense, a Wiccan tradition is a map pointing out a specific route to the Goddess.

Part III of this book consists of a guide to creating a new Wiccan tradition, one perfectly suited for you. In writing it yourself, you can focus it toward your personal needs, and the end result may well be far more spiritually satisfying than any other Wiccan tradition.

It's never necessary to take on this task. However, if you do decide to create your own tradition, this and the following chapters will present you with some ideas to help you get started.

WHY CREATE A TRADITION?

Why not? Few published Books of Shadows are complete, and virtually all are designed for group worship. Thus, none are ideally suited to the Solitary practitioner. This alone is reason enough to create your own Wiccan tradition.

Additionally, the published sets of rituals may seem distant, or foreign, or they may not move you to fully involve yourself in Wicca. You also may have far too many questions regarding a specific Wiccan tradition, even one that has been published, to adequately perform its rites.

Then again, a creative streak may be moving within you, searching for an outlet. Creating a Wiccan Tradition is a creative process, but it must be done with control.

HOW TO BEGIN

Right now, as you're reading this, grab a pen and several sheets of paper. On the top of the first page, write the following in large letters:

DEITY CONCEPTS

On the second, write TOOLS, ALTARS, DRESS, JEWELRY

On the third, RITUALS

On the fourth, BELIEFS

On the fifth, RULES

On the six, SYMBOLS AND RUNES

On the seventh, THE BOOK OF SHADOWS

Use these pages to make rough notes while reading the following chapters. Later, you'll probably need far more room for your thoughts and notes on each subject, but this is a fine start. (Utilizing a computer or a typewriter, at this early stage, might slow you down.)

The important part is to start actually putting thoughts into words on a page. These will eventually evolve into rituals, beliefs, rules and other things. A Wiccan tradition isn't misty or ethereal; it possesses specifics, and to create a Wiccan tradition you must first determine these specifics.

Wicca isn't a spiritual free-for-all. A true Wiccan tradition must be based upon Wiccan conventions. Though there's plenty of room for personal touches, some things are essentially Wiccan and can't be discarded. These will be clearly pointed out.

In the following chapters we'll be exploring one method of creating a Wiccan tradition. You're free to use it if it feels right; if it doesn't, don't. And if you don't wish to begin a new path, feel free not to.

Creating your own Wiccan tradition is exciting and challenging. It's a process of defining not only your means of spiritual expression, but also the nature of your spirituality itself. Thus, it's a journey of self-discovery.

14: DEITY CONCEPTS

Without deities, there would be no religions of any kind. How do you, personally, define the Deity concepts of your tradition? Every Wiccan possesses her or his own conceptions of the Goddess and God. We built these up through personal experience and interactions with Them as well as through research. Such images will, naturally, form the basis of your new tradition's Deity concepts. Research will also provide assistance. (See Suggested Reading at the end of this chapter.) The nature of your tradition's Deities is of great importance, as we'll see.

THE GODDESS AND THE GOD

Worship is at the heart of any religion, and it's important to firm your conceptions of the Goddess and God. If, up to this point, they've been like astral grandparents, or powerful but misty beings, it might be time to mentally bring them down to Earth.

The following notes can be used in sharpening your conceptions of the Goddess and God. These, combined with the readings listed at the end of this chapter and your own spiritual experiences, should allow you to gain a greater understanding of the Goddess and God.*

*Until recently, Wicca possessed few teachings concerning the Goddess and God. We gleaned what we could from the few myths (sacred stories) that were taught to us; from verbal teachings, personal experience and the hints provided by other Wiccans, but we had little upon which to base our conceptions save for personal experience. Today, however, renewed research and interest in Goddess worship and in pre-Christian religions in general has offered us much information, some of which we can utilize and frame within a Wiccan context. See the Bibliography.

THE GODDESS

The Goddess is, truly, all things. She's all power, all wisdom, all love, all fertility, all creativity; the nurturing as well as destructive force Who created our universe and Who shapes our lives.

This may be your concept of the Goddess: She Who Is All. Even so, you'll probably need to determine Her symbols and some of Her specific manifestations to adequately connect with Her. In other words, you'll have to discover Her private telephone number; Her personal portrait of power which, through ritual, will facilitate communication.

(The below list is merely a short catalog of a few of the Goddess' attributes. Please understand that these are aspects of the same being, The Goddess, and is far from a complete listing.)

Here are some clues to determining Her nature:

- Goddess of outer space.
  Goddess of the stars.
  Goddess of galaxies.
  Goddess of the Universe.

- Goddess of the Moon.
  Goddess of the Waxing Moon.
  Goddess of the Full Moon.
  Goddess of the Waning Moon.

- Goddess of the Earth.
  Goddess of earth fertility and of plants.
  Goddess of the animals.
  Goddess of storms, earthquakes, volcanic activity.
  Goddess of gentle rain, wells, rivers, lakes, seas and oceans.

- Goddess of freshness, renewal, beginnings, promise and potential.

- ✪ Goddess of childbirth, mothers and mothering.

- ✪ Goddess of love, beauty, compassion.

- ✪ Goddess of healing.

- ✪ Goddess of prophecy.

- ✪ Goddess of magic.

- ✪ Goddess of wisdom.

- ✪ Goddess of power.

- ✪ Goddess of destruction, retribution, war.*

A space goddess isn't a truly Wiccan concept. At least two more aspects must be added: Goddess of the Moon and the Earth. Indeed, most Wiccan conceptions of the Goddess are built upon the many combinations possible between these aspects. This signifies a Goddess related to everything, Whose closest symbols are the Moon and the Earth beneath our feet. Everything on the Earth and of the Earth is under Her domain.

Most Wiccans also acknowledge the Goddess' role in childbirth, healing, love; as the provider of wisdom and the sender of magical energy in times of need.

One conception of the Goddess has become quite popular. As the Triple Goddess (related to the phases of the moon), She's most closely linked with the New Moon and with freshness (in Her Maiden aspect); the Full Moon, mothers and childbirth (as The Mother); and the Waning Moon with wisdom, prophecy, magic, destruction and retribution (The Crone; source of all wisdom). What I might be forgiven for terming The Goddess of the Three Aspects is directly linked with women's lives and

---

*I'm aware that there are many other types of Goddesses. However, I'm limited here by those that have been either worshipped or acknowledged in contemporary Wicca. Pagan isn't necessarily Wiccan.

cycles and, thus, has become enormously popular both within and without Wicca proper. (See Suggested Readings.) (Some Wiccans seem to believe that this is the only conception of the Goddess that has ever existed. It certainly isn't, but is currently a quite popular Wiccan model.)

Most Wiccans acknowledge that the Goddess possesses a dark side. This is evident from nature itself: storms and earthquakes immediately come to mind. However, we've chosen not to focus on these aspects, and never invoke Her for such purposes. Let's face it: the last thing we need is to bring more destruction and violence into the world. If She sees fit to do so, fine; the same isn't true for humans.

In Wiccan workings, we look to the more uplifting aspects of the Goddess. To do otherwise would lead to misery and despair. If our religion is to provide us with spiritual refreshment, hope and love, we should focus on the Goddess as a being of love, compassion, nurturing and wonder. I'd rather worship Her in this guise than as a Warrior Queen, for I'm not a warrior, we've had far too many wars, and I have no wish to indirectly encourage any others.*

One of the aspects missing from my list is the Goddess of Fate. Wiccans rarely invoke Her in this way, simply because we don't believe in predestination. If we did, we wouldn't practice magic to alter our lives, for it wouldn't be effective. However, some Wiccans may argue that the Goddess does, indeed, have plans for us, and that She can set up situations that will gently remind us of our lessons, or that will sway us to make correct decisions in times of stress. In this way, perhaps, the Goddess can indeed be

---

*Many of you will disagree with me, especially those of you who work outside strict Wiccan practice. I'll admit that, yes, there may come a time when we must invoke The Lady of Justice, but such worship can become disheartening and even dangerous. Only she or he who is innocent of wrong-doing should dare to invoke this aspect of the Goddess, for She'll probably bring justice to the wrong-doer, even if it's Her worshipper. Think carefully concerning this.

seen as a Goddess of Fate, but not in the normally understood sense of the word. We don't do the Goddess' will; She always gives us options, and allows us to fall on our faces if (when) we take the wrong course.

As the Goddess of healing, love, beauty, compassion and prophecy, She's worshipped by nearly all Wiccans. Some emphasize these attributes, at least when in need of them. However, She's always a goddess of love and concern, and healing rituals directed to or through Her will receive Her blessing.

It's time to discuss the many forms that the Goddess may assume. You may have already seen Her in meditations, dreams, and during rituals. If so, think about how She appeared to you. She is the One with the Thousand Forms, and that which She revealed to you is a valuable tool in contacting her at later times.

If you haven't physically seen the Goddess yet (and many Wiccans have never seen Her), don't despair. It may occur. While waiting, build up your own image of the Goddess, using your feelings, intuitions and perceptions of Her. (Remember that she may secretly assist in this process.)

Some Wiccans see Her in quite specific ways:

"I see the Goddess as a rounded, earthy goddess-woman with hair the color of wheat, eyes as blue as the ocean, skin as dark as the rich black soil; naked, holding flowers in Her outstretched hands, standing beneath a tree and smiling."

"I see the Goddess as a celestial lunar being. Her skin is milky white (as it would appear by moonlight); She wears a white diaphanous robe that doesn't conceal Her body, which changes its shape with the Moon's phase; a necklace of pearls and moonstones encircles Her neck and an upturned crescent rests on Her forehead. Her hair is white (or silver or blonde) and She tosses the glowing Moon between Her hands."

"I see the Goddess as my late grandmother: dressed in old-fashioned clothes that She's made with Her hands, seated in a rocking chair by a fire of willow branches in a house without walls. She's slowly stitching a design of the universe on a dark blue cloth and tells me all the secrets as I sit near Her feet on a rag rug. She is the Crone."

These are highly personal visions of the Goddess. None are incorrect; these and many others are accepted by Wiccans.

Some Wiccan's conceptions may be closer to those formed in other cultures: "I see the Goddess as Athena, of the hunt." "I see the Goddess as Spider Grandmother." "As Diana." "Isis." "Hecate." (Photos of statues and other images of the goddess can be found in a number of books; see Suggested Reading at the end of this chapter.)

Again, it may be enough for you to feel Her presence. If you've already formed an image of the Goddess (or, putting it another way, if She has already revealed Her form to you), fine. If not, you may wish to discover Her form through ritual work, prayer and, perhaps, dreams.

One word of warning: if you've already developed a clear picture of the Goddess, and have already determined Her aspects, don't let the above information alter this. Hold fast to that which you discover; it's of the highest rarity and value.

Divine symbolism is another aspect of your personal conception of the Goddess. These include both those used in Her worship and those directly or indirectly related to Her.

This is in part determined by your understanding of the Goddess. If She's primarily linked with the Moon, symbols representing the Earth wouldn't speak of Her. Here are some suggested symbols of the types of Goddesses listed above, to be used in ritual design, poems, chants and invocations:

- Goddess of Outer Space. (Darkness; black cloth; stars; the night; the void; cauldron; nocturnal flowers and owls.)

- Goddess of the Moon. (Crescents; pearls; moonstones; mirror; silver; labrys.)

- Goddess of the Earth. (Fruits; plants, especially grains; fertilizing nature; corn dollies; Goddess animals such as cats, dolphins, lions, horses, dogs, bees; pure water; a shell collected on a beach; cups, chalices, cauldrons; emeralds.)

- Goddess of freshness, renewal, beginnings, promise and potential. (Unplowed fields; eggs; spring; New Moon.)

- Goddess of childbirth, mothers and mothering. (Full Moon; holed stones; round or oval-shaped objects; a baby.)

- Goddess of love, beauty, compassion. (Mirrors; hearts; flowers; honey.)

- Goddess of healing. (Purifying waters; power streaming hands.)

- Goddess of prophecy. (Quartz crystal; psychic awareness; caves; nudity; pools of water.)

- Goddess of magic. (All magical tools; sword; athame; spindle; fire; cauldron.)

- Goddess of wisdom. (Fires; books; owls; Waning Moon.)

- Goddesses of destruction, retribution, war. (Not recommended.)

Keep in mind that such symbols may not be actually used in ritual, but can be utilized when writing ritual invocations. The mention of these tools immediately and directly connects your invocation with the Goddess.

Many other symbols and tools are connected with the Goddess in general and in Her particular aspects.

THE GOD

The God shares an equal place in the hearts of most Wiccans, for without Him, our world would be cold, desolate of fertility and all life. Though most Wiccans don't experience as emotional a response to the God as they do to the Goddess, he's certainly called upon in times of need (particularly for protection) Here are some attributes of the God in Wiccan thought:

- God of the Sun.

- God of human fertility (and, thus, sex).

- God of the Earth.
  God of wild animals.
  God of crops.
  God of deserts, plains, valleys.

- God of Summer.

- God of hunting.

- God of death and rebirth.

- God of retribution, war and conflicts.

This list pretty well sums the main aspects of the God in Wiccan thought. The God simply hasn't accumulated as many Wiccan-acknowledged aspects as has the Goddess. There are certainly many other aspects of the God (for example, as the inventor of tools; overseer of competitions, and so on) that haven't been adopted by Wiccans. This has resulted in a dearth of Wiccan mythic material involving the God.

Some recent authors (see readings) have tried to fill this void with rituals and myths concerning the Oak King and the Ivy King. This concept is now quite common, at least at public rituals and among some Solitary Wiccans. However, I know little of it, and direct the interested reader to the appropriate book by the Farrars (see readings).

Let's speak frankly here. The Goddess appears to be more loving, more understanding and caring than the God. The God, through no fault of His own, may appear to be unapproachable except in Wiccan ritual, and even then formalized prayers are necessary. This is a natural human reaction, even among Wiccans, and easily explains the lack of material regarding Him.

One of the underlying reasons for this problem isn't difficult to discover. Many new Wiccans have difficulty in approaching the God. For their entire lives, they've been taught that there's only one God. He's jealous, angry and promises we'll all end up in a place of darkness and suffering after death. Vivid portraits of His wrath were firmly imprinted in many children's minds at a quite impressionable age, and it can be difficult for some of these persons, now grown and entering Wicca, to remove such lingering conceptions of male Deity.

Then again, some feminists wish to direct their worship solely to the Goddess. Many of them have, quite frankly, had enough of male spiritual conceptions and have no desire to attune with them in Wicca. For them, worship of the Goddess is completely fulfilling and, except when trying to adapt Goddess-God rituals to strictly Goddess rites, they find few challenges in solely honoring the Goddess in Wiccan rites.

The God has been given a bad name by 2,000 years of patriarchal hyperbole that has strayed far off the path that Jesus allegedly once preached. Religious institutions have transformed the male conception of Deity into a wrathful being whose followers have wiped out entire civilizations and destroyed hundreds of cultures; a God in whose name millions of persons have been killed in holy wars; a God whose representatives have repeatedly stated that Deity is not female and that women cannot possibly achieve a rapport with the Divine to the extent that they should be allowed to be priests; a male Deity ruling over a male-oriented world in which men have long used religion as an excuse to dominate, subdue and abuse women.

In this long, bitter and inexcusably violent period of our species' short history, the male Deity has been given a negative, frightening image. We know him only as the god of vengeance and war. True, this god is nice to his worshippers, but any who don't worship Him, or who don't limit their worship to Him, are doomed to spend eternity in a pit of fire and torture, with no hope of another life or escape.

It isn't surprising, then, that many new Wiccans don't feel comfortable with the Wiccan concept of God, at least during their first ventures into Wiccan. Women may have a particularly difficult time. While they may be surprised and delighted to have found a religion that embraces women, that acknowledges their inner power and spiritual strength, that allows them to participate as leaders in ritual and that – incredibly – actually worships a Goddess, they may not quite be able to bring the God into their rites. It can be difficult to forget 20, 30 or 40 years of negative God Imagery.

Some Wiccans eventually adjust and have no difficulty in worshipping both the Goddess and the God in Wiccan ritual. Others decide to worship only the Goddess. (These are personal decisions but, once again, I'll state the party line: Wicca consists of the worship of the Goddess *and* the God.)

I've found in my own experience that those who come to Wicca having never truly believed in or practiced any other religion have no problems including the God in their rites. Additionally, even many who did emerge from conventional religious backgrounds experience no difficulty with the concept of the God.

To be old-fashioned, traditional Wicca, your rites should honor both. This may necessitate rediscovering the God by expanding your awareness of His presence and of His attributes. Below are some ideas.

Do you see the God as woman-hating? See Him instead as a being that the Goddess has brought into Her arms. Remember that thousands of priestesses worship Him every day. Invoke Him to assist in the furtherance of women's rights. Ask yourself how can any true conception of Deity can hate its children.

Do you see the God as bringer of death? Remember that death is necessary at some point, and that the Goddess brings us rebirth.

Do you see the God as the bringer of war? Recall that men have simply exploited His dark side for this purpose. Remember, however, that war is rarely religious in nature: it's main motivations are politics and money. Religion is often simply an excuse.

Do you see the God as a judge, as the caster-down of human souls into hell? Wiccans don't accept the existence of hell; no one casts us down anywhere, and the God unconditionally loves us.

Do you see God as a frightening, unknowable spirit hovering around the Earth? See Him, instead, in faces of your male friends and in the eyes of young boys. See Him in freshly-baked bread; in bunches of grapes; in towering, snow-capped mountains; in the Sun that warms the Earth and provides us our food and all of our tools for living.

I hope that these ideas provide some assistance to those who find it difficult to contact the God. This is a major problem and is one of the reasons why Goddess spirituality is so prevalent today: over the centuries, men have changed a gentle fertility god into a blood-thirsty monster. Erase such images and concentrate on the God's other aspects.

Again, you may have already seen the God in a vision, dream or meditation. He may have appeared in the incense smoke during ritual. If not, He may well yet make Himself visible to you.

Here are some Wiccan's visualizations of the God:

"He stands on a hill, naked, His skin reddish-brown from sunlight. His hair is long and black, and no razor has touched His chin or cheeks. He holds a shimmering golden knife; below Him are heaped piles of grain and vegetables."

"He 's dressed in a brown, rustic tunic, holding a baby in one hand and the hand of an aged woman in the other. Dried flowers – symbolic of both fertility and its end – are entwined in His beard. He stands between light and darkness."

"The God is dressed in furs, but is bare foot. As I see Him among a forest of trees he wears horns on His head and a stag follows nearby. A bow is slung over one shoulder; a spear is in His hand. The aggressive expression on His face is softened by His caring eyes."

Again, some see the God in the terms of cultural concepts: "I see him as Pan." "The God appears to me as Grandfather." "As Belinus." "Osiris". "Apollo".

There are symbols that Wiccans use to represent the God in creating ritual and poetry. As you might imagine, there are fewer of these symbols than for the Goddess.

- God of the Sun. (Sun; gold; brass; bonfires; candles.)

- God of human fertility. (Acorns; pine cones; wands.)

- God of the Earth. (Grain; stones; valleys; seeds; forests; bull, snake, fish, wolf, eagle, lizard.)

- God of Summer. (Blazing fires; daylight; the South.)

- God of hunting. (Horns; spears; quiver; bow; arrows.)

- God of death and rebirth. (Sunset; winter; pomegranates; dried leaves; sickle; night; the West.)

○ God of retribution, war and conflicts. (Best not to invoke this attribute.)

Remember: the God is just as much a part of contemporary Paganism as is the Goddess. He isn't fearsome unless you decide to focus on his fearsome attributes. (This is also true of the Goddess.) He can be the epitome of compassion, caring, nurturing maleness, but only you can discover this.

AFTERWORD

I've got this nagging thought that my references to seeing the Goddess and God may make some of you feel left out. Don't worry about it. By the word 'see', I don't mean that, while completely awake, we look up and notice that the Goddess is physically standing in the room before us. Visitations of that magnitude are so rare that we needn't wait around for them.

We have better opportunities for seeing the Goddess and God during alternate states of consciousness. In the circle, when we're in ritual consciousness, we're far more likely to see Them. We may also get glimpses, as I've already said, during dreams and meditations.

The first time I saw the Goddess was in a circle. I was seated before the altar and was meditating on Her. It can happen, but don't expect to use your eyes to see the forms of the Goddess and God. Realize, too, that the forms in which They come to you may be quite different from those that They present to others.

SUGGESTED READING

The Goddess:

There are simply too many books to list, and more are being released every day. Many of the new Goddess books aren't Wiccan in nature. I've largely tried to restrict myself here to Wiccan Goddess writings (or to those that have most profoundly affected Wiccan thought). For a wide variety of other titles, check the women's studies sections of virtually any new book store.

Farrar and Farrar, *The Witches' Goddess.* (The entire book.)

Graves, *The White Goddess.* (The entire book. Goddess speculations, poetry and mythic information that has had a tremendous impact on contemporary Wicca.)

Neumann, *The Great Mother: An Analysis of the Archetype.* (The entire book. A Jungian-based look at the Goddess. Zillions of photos of Goddess images.)

Walker, Barbara, *The Women's Encyclopedia of Myths and Secrets.* (Many of her research sources are highly questionable, but this remains a good encyclopedic look at women and goddesses.)

The God:

Farrar and Farrar, *Eight Sabbats for Witches.* (Information concerning the Oak King and the Holly King is scattered throughout this book.)

Farrar and Farrar, *The Witches' God.* (The entire book. Oak King and Holly King information can be found on pp. 35-38.)

Starhawk, *The Spiral Dance* (Pages 93-107 offer a somewhat feminist view of the God.)

Cunningham, *Wicca: A Guide for the Solitary Practitioner*. (Pages 12-14.)

15: TOOLS, ALTARS, DRESS AND RITUAL JEWELRY

TOOLS

Most Wiccan traditions use the same tools, with a few additions among certain groups. Since the tools are virtually mandatory in Wiccan ritual, you won't have to spend hours deciding on which to include in your new tradition. However, you can determine the exact forms of these tools, their symbolism and ritual uses.

For review, these are the main Wiccan tools:

- *Images of the Goddess and God.* Many traditions place them on the altar. The nature of these images are of great variety. Some simply use candles; others natural objects representative of the Goddess and God. Still other Wiccans use hand-crafted sculptures or drawings. Genuine clay is available that, when dried in a normal oven, becomes quite hard. It can be used to create your own interpretations of the Goddess and God (good ideas for designs can be found in archaeological books).

- *The Book of Shadows.* This hand-written book records the heart of any Wiccan tradition: rites, rules, magical techniques and other information. (See Chapter 21.)

- *The Athame* (black-handled knife). A director of energy used to create the magic circle.

- *The Censer*. In It, incense or herbs are burned to invite the presence of the Goddess and God, and to cleanse the ritual space. (A small box, bowl or bottle to contain the unburned incense is also used.)

- *The Cup (or Chalice)*. This holds wine, water or other liquids for use during ritual.

- *The White-Handled Knife*. This is used for actual cutting purposes either within or within and without the circle.

- *Salt*. Generally used for circle casting, consecration of tools and for other purposes.

- *Water*. For purification of the circle.

- *The Pentacle*. This is a flat disk or plate bearing, at the least, the symbol of a five-pointed star.

- *The Wand*. A traditional tool, it's generally used in either power-raising or while inviting beings to attend the circle.

I've listed the tools here because they're an integral part of Wicca, and all Wiccan tradition should utilize most if not all of them. Why? Because the tools are among the outer aspects of Wicca by which we define our religion. If you created a tradition that never utilized any of these tools, it probably wouldn't be Wiccan. Hence, the tools should be used unless you decide to forge out on your own.

Other tools that aren't as widely used can be incorporated into your Wiccan tradition as you see fit.

- *The Cauldron.* Some Wiccans utilize cauldrons as symbols of the Goddess, and they can be the center of religious rites. Fires are sometimes lit within them.

- *The Bell.* Bells can be rung at specific points in rituals.

- *The Broom.* My first teacher always cleansed the ritual area with her broom before ritual.

- *The Cords.* Of importance in initiatory groups, in which cords often symbolize the bond of love and responsibility shared by the members, cords are also used in some initiation rites. Cords can certainly be used by the Solitary Wiccan, but needn't be constantly on the altar. The cords are truly tools of coven workings.

- *Altar Cloth.* Some Wiccan traditions prescribe a specific color altar cloth for use on the altar. Certain designs (such as pentagrams) may be embroidered or painted onto these cloths. Many traditions, however, don't use them. (My first teacher usually used white cloths on the altar for Full Moons. I honestly can't remember [after all, this was 21 years ago] whether we used cloths for the Sabbats.)

Such tool lists can be extended: bottles of ritual oils, candle snuffers, incense spoons and swords immediately come to mind. Other objects may well be on the altar with the other tools from time to time: flowers or seasonal greens, sketches or runes or photographs for magical purposes.

In deciding which tools to use in your new tradition, always rely on your experience. You may read that the athame should be double-edged in one source; in another, single-edged. Some books state that the athame must be razor-sharp, while others say that it can be dull. You must decide what's right for you. Make a decision and keep it.

Put all such decisions in writing, first in rough notes and eventually in your Book of Shadows (see Chapter 21). You may well write in your Book of Shadows, "The athame – a double-edged, black-handled, hilted knife used for power-direction. It need not be sharp." This, then, will become part of your tradition.

ALTARS

As the physical center of your religious observances, the altar is of prime importance. Theories concerning the significance of and the proper arrangement of tools on altars vary. That altars are necessary, however, is rarely questioned. Once again, altars don't necessarily make the Wiccan, but the use of such altars is one of the defining yardsticks of Wiccan practices.

However much we may enjoy spontaneous rituals in a moonlit forest, while watching a desert sunset or lying on a grassy plain, structured rituals are an important part of long-standing Wiccan tradition, and structured rituals (more often than not) are performed with altars.

Many books contain altar designs and layouts that you can use to create your own. As most Wiccan traditions utilize a specific altar arrangement, so too can your tradition. Here are some basics:

- The altar is always round. The altar is always square. The altar is always rectangular. The altar can be of any shape. This pretty much sums Wiccan thought regarding the appropriate shape of the altar. Many use round altars to symbolize, among other matters, the Goddess. Make your decision.

- The Image or symbol of the Goddess can be placed to the left of the altar as you stand before it; the image of the God to the right.

○ Tools associated with the Goddess (the chalice, bells, sistrums, brooms, cauldrons) are often placed to the left. Tools associated with the God (swords, wands, the white-handled knife, bowl of salt, the censer) are often placed to the right on the altar. Other tools may be placed in the center: the pentacle, the censer, fresh flowers or greens.

○ A totally different method of arranging the altar takes the elements into account. Earthy tools (pentacle, salt) are placed to the North; the censer and incense to the East to represent Air; a red candle to the South and the bowl of water, chalice, cauldron, bell and other tools to the West. (This and the above system can't be used simultaneously, and neither is more correct.)

○ Candles are usually placed where they can't easily be knocked over, such as to the rear of the altar.

○ Leave space on your altar for your opened Book of Shadows. If not, create or find a small stand on which to place the Book during rituals. Though our rituals should be memorized, we can all have lapses of memory and it's nice to have a reminder close at hand.

○ The altar is sacred. Not that the Goddess and God live within it, but because we utilize it and the tools that it bears for spiritual purposes. Thus, only objects directly connected with Wicca and/or magical rites performed in the circle should be placed on the altar.

○ If, after ritual, the altar is used for other purposes (as, perhaps, a coffee table), at such times it ceases to be an altar. Only when it's covered with the tools of our religion and used as a focal point for ritual does it become an altar.

From these generalities, and by studying the sample altar designs included in other Wiccan books, you should be able to come up with a suitable design for your tradition. Include a sketch or a diagram of your altar design in the Book of Shadows.

Be certain that you know the *whys* of your arrangement. If you decide to place the athame directly in front of a goddess image, with its point directed at Her symbol, know why you've decided to do this.

ROBES

Many Wiccans dress in special robes for worship. Such garments are usually worn solely for ritual observances, and may be plain or decorated with symbols or embroidery.

Some Wiccans worship naked. This is a personal decision. Though a robe might seem to be useless to a Solitary Wiccan that practices ritual nudity, it's still good to have a robe around somewhere, in case you ever change your mind, or are invited to a robed ritual. It does happen.

Patterns for robes can be found in most yardage shops. If you make your own, use natural cloth. Polyester and other synthetic fabrics will leave you hot and uncomfortable in circle, and will hardly connect you with the Deities of nature.

Robes are also available at many occult shops and from mail-order businesses.

RITUAL JEWELRY

By ritual jewelry I'm not referring to rings and necklaces worn on a daily basis, even if they're symbolic of the Goddess and/or God. This term refers to jewelry worn only in the circle for ritual purposes.

In many Wiccan traditions, a necklace is considered the ideal piece of ritual jewelry for women, for it symbolizes reincarnation as well as the Goddess. Some traditions virtually demand that women wear a necklace of some type in the circle.

Other traditions may use bracelets (usually flat and inscribed with runes or symbols) or rings in ritual. The famous garter is usually worn only by High Priestesses of certain traditions.

You can simply wear whatever you wish in the circle. Alternately, you may wear a special piece of jewelry that you specifically dedicate to your tradition, or may even state in the Book of Shadows that a certain piece of jewelry (such as a moonstone ring) should be worn in the circle at all times.

If you're expert at jewelry making you may create a unique piece: a beaded necklace, a ring or pendant created by the lost-wax method.

Remember: ritual jewelry isn't worn outside the circle. When it is, it loses its specialness and its direct links with ritual. Other pieces can be worn around the clock, but if you choose to use ritual jewelry, save it for the circle.

16: RITUAL DESIGN PART I

R ituals will certainly be an important part of your new tradition. Thus, we'll be spending some time discussing their creation. Save in rare cases (emergencies), or during spontaneous rites, all Wiccan rituals should include the following:

- Purification of Self

- Purification of Space

- Creation of Sacred Space (including the altar)

- Invocation

- Ritual Observance (and/or) Raising of Energy

- Earthing the Power

- Thanking the Goddess and God

- Breaking the Circle

As you well know, ritual observances certainly aren't necessary during every single Wiccan ritual, and neither is energy raising (magic). They're done when appropriate. However, the remaining ritual aspects are vitally necessary if your tradition's rituals are to be Wiccan.

The exact ways in which you observe these ritual necessities are, of course, up to you. Following is the way one Solitary Wiccan might construct her or his basic rituals (allowing for changes depending on the occasion):

- Purification of Self (bathe and/or anoint with oil)

- Purification of Space (sprinkle fresh water or sweep area)

- Creation of Sacred Space (set up altar; cast circle with athame; carry around salt, censer, candle and water)

- Invocation (pray to the Goddess and God, either with memorized invocations or with spontaneous words)

- Ritual Observance (perform rituals recorded in the Book of Shadows, if a Sabbat or Esbat)

- Raising of Energy (this Wiccan has chosen not to do so on the Sabbats, but performs magic on the Full Moons)

- Earthing the Power (eating crackers and drinking wine, milk or water)

- Thanking the Goddess and God (in spontaneous words or written words)

- Breaking the Circle (cut circle with athame, draw energy back into the knife; dissemble the altar)

This is one method of fulfilling the basic requirements for a Wiccan ritual. Once you've found your own, discover precisely how these elements can be fit together in order to create a flowing ritual.

ESBATS

Generally speaking, any Wiccan ritual held at any time other than a Sabbat is an Esbat. Full Moon rituals are Esbats, but they aren't the only Esbats. Some traditions hold circles on the New Moons as well. These, too, are Esbats.

There are many reasons to observe Esbats. You may wish to talk to the Goddess, and there's no better place to do so than safely within a circle. You may have an urgent magical need (such as a friend's sickness) that demands a circle be held and power raised within it.

And, like most Wiccans, you simply may wish to re-experience the serene, otherworldly atmosphere of the circle. That's okay too.

Many Esbats aren't pre-planned. Still, virtually all follow the basic ritual format outlined above, with one exception: ritual observances aren't held, and magic may or may not be made. Other than that, it's the same.

Full Moon rituals are a bit different. As you well know, most Full Moon rituals observed in Wicca today are held, naturally enough, on the Full Moon. If this isn't possible, two days prior to or two days after the actual phase is considered to be close enough to the time. Here's one suggested plan for a Full Moon Esbat:

- Have a purification bath.

- Fumigate the room in which the Esbat is to be held with a mixture of sandalwood and frankincense burning on incense charcoal.

- Create the altar with the usual tools. (Some Wiccans use a slightly different altar arrangement for the Esbats; others use the same plan for all rites. Additional tools, connecting this occasion with the Moon, may include white altar cloths, silver objects, crescent moons, moonstone, white flowers and other lunar objects.)

- Circle casting. (This usually isn't different from that used in Sabbat rituals.)

- The Goddess (and usually, the God) are asked to be present at the circle.

○ The Goddess is invoked in a fairly long, flowery chant that acknowledges Her and connects Her with the Moon (though we don't specifically pray *to* the Moon). This period of invocation may, alternately, consist of a song either sung or played on an instrument; a dance; even a series of properly lunar gestures.

○ Following this invocation, some Wiccans then meditate upon the Moon itself or upon a Goddess image (but such meditation may come later).

○ Then, after the meditation, or in its place, a work of magic may be performed, to take advantage of the Moon's more powerful force. (We don't necessarily take lunar energy directly from the Moon. But just as the Moon rules the tides, so too does it rule the tides of our bodily energy. At its full, the Moon subtly increases the amount of energy available from our bodies, thus making magic performed during this phase that much more powerful. Women whose menstruation coincides with the Full Moon may be doubly or triply empowered.)

○ After the energy has been raised and sent toward its destination, many Wiccans will sit, meditate, pray or simply relax.

○ Next, the Wiccan grounds herself or himself by eating the traditional crescent-shaped cakes* and by sipping wine, apple cider, lemonade or juice.

---

*For a tasty recipe, see Wicca: A Guide for the Solitary Practitioner, p. 152.

○ Finally, the Goddess and God are thanked for attending the rites, the circle is broken, and the altar tools are safely put away.

This general Full-Moon ritual structure can be personalized in many ways, according to your desires and spiritual needs. You may wish to jot down some ideas for your own Full Moon rituals.

Invocations can be obtained from a number of books (see the reading list at the end of this chapter), and you can use any that appeal to you. For the Full Moon, however, use only those that invoke the Goddess in Her lunar aspect.

You may also wish to create your own invocations. The best are in rhyme, or in carefully-constructed, soothing, flowing language.

SABBATS

Sabbats are quite different. As you've probably seen from reading published Sabbat rituals, there's little agreement as to each holiday's meanings and appropriate ritual actions. Some Sabbat rites have been heavily influenced by a specific culture; others are more generic. Certain Sabbat ritual cycles are directly related to a tradition's sacred stories concerning the Goddess and God; in other traditions, little mythic information is evident in the Sabbat scripts.

In any case, most published Sabbat rituals are designed for groups. Since you can't be at two places at once in the circle, it's difficult to act out seasonal plays, or to respond to your own statements, without feeling quite silly. What to do? Write your own.

Keep these things in mind:

Wicca's vaguely British/Middle Eastern cultural framework can be used to determine Sabbat themes (and often is). These include: birth of the God (sun) at Yule; the Goddess' recovery at Imbolc; the coming of

Spring (Ostara); the mating or wedding of the Goddess and God (Beltane); the coming of Summer (Litha); the first harvest (Lughnasadh); the final harvest (Mabon); the death of the God (Samhain).

There are few other options. You may create your own mythic story of the Goddess and the God (intertwined with the seasons, the Sun and the Moon) based on the below list of basic, seasonal symbolism of the Sabbats:

- *Yule*: renewal and rebirth during winter

- *Imbolc*: the festival of lights (to encourage the sun's return)

- *Ostara*: The start of Spring

- *Beltane*: The return of full-blown fertility

- *Litha*: Great, magical power

- *Lughnasadh*: Harvest and thanksgiving

- *Mabon*: Second harvest and mysteries

- *Samhain*: the end of Summer; the dead are honored

In your new myth, each Sabbat should, in light of Wiccan tradition, have something to do with the actual agricultural and/or astronomical phenomena that are then occurring. To ignore this would be to deny the night's (or day's) special power. This would invalidate any reason for a ritual's observance. In other words: don't stray too far from the path. Frankly, it's best to utilize traditional Sabbat symbolism and to write new rituals that celebrate this heritage.

The basic structure of Sabbat rites can be divided into two parts: spoken words and ritual actions. The spoken words are nearly always directly related to the Sabbat. The Goddess is invoked on Imbolc as the Lady of Fertility; farewells are said to the God at Samhain. Additionally, words may be spoken by the Wiccan of the internal changes that occur at the Sabbats.

In creating your own tradition, you may choose to use appropriate passages from published Sabbat rituals. Alternately, you may write your own words. The second method is certainly best, but many beautiful Sabbat prayers and words have been printed, and I see no reason why you shouldn't incorporate them in your new tradition If you're comfortable in doing so, and if the words move you. That's what's important.

Ritual actions are just as important a part of Sabbats as are words. Here are some familiar ones for each holiday*:

- ✪ *Yule:* Fires are lit within cauldrons; candles may be carried around the circle; trees or potted evergreens may be honored as symbols of continuing fertility of the Earth; a Yule log may be lit if a fire is physically within the circle.

- ✪ *Imbolc:* candles or torches are lit and held in circle, and are usually carried around the altar at some point; symbol of the wheel is placed on the altar; ritual blessing and planting of seeds in pots in the circle with requests to the Goddess and God.

- ✪ *Ostara:* A fire is lit in the circle with appropriate words during the rite itself – not before.

- ✪ *Beltane:* weaving ribbons (not traditional, but a solitary version of creating and dancing the May pole); bonfire leaping; the blowing of horns.

These basic ritual actions have been culled from many books of shadows.

- *Midsummer:* cauldron, ringed with flowers (or filled with fresh water and flowers); sword plunged into cauldron; bonfire leaping; drying herbs over the balefire.

- *Lughnasadh:* bread is eaten, tossed into flames, or otherwise used in ritual; wheat may be woven into Goddess images or symbols.

- *Mabon:* fruit is praised as proof of the Goddess' and God's love; a ritual sprinkling of leaves.

- *Samhain:* scrying in smoke, candle flame or fire; calling the departed ones; leaving food outside after ritual for the dead.

There are symbols, specialized tools and colors associated with each Sabbat that can also be used to create the Sabbat rites of your new tradition. Here's a list of some of these:

- *Yule:* The colors are green and red. A wheel symbol (which can easily be made from a wreath or a wreath form; use your imagination); evergreens; Yule log; small tree (potted).

- *Imbolc:* The colors are white, or green and white, or blue. A dish of snow; evergreens; candles.

- *Ostara:* The color is white. A potted plant; cauldron or bonfire.

- Beltane: The color is white. Fresh flowers; cauldron filled with flowers. Mirrors are also appropriate.

- *Litha:* The color is white. Mugwort. Mirrors to capture the sun (or the flames of the fire).

- *Lughnasadh:* The colors are red and orange. Corn dollies; special loaves of bread; grain.

- *Maybon:* The colors are red and brown. Pine cones; acorns; wheat; dried leaves.

- *Samhain:* The colors are red or black. Pomegranates; pumpkins; apples.

You may wish to follow the below plan in creating your tradition's Sabbat rituals.

- Write the name of each Sabbat on a separate piece of paper.

- Jot down notes regarding each Sabbat's significance (see reading list at the end of this chapter)

- Decide which of these influences is of special importance; the ones that seem to flow from one Sabbat to another.

- Begin with Yule. Read every ritual that you can find for this Sabbat. Afterward, leave the books open to the correct pages and study the rituals together. What are their common themes? Which structures or ritual actions do you enjoy the most? Next, read the lists of ritual actions and ritual symbols I've given above. On the page entitled 'Yule', write down your choices of Yule actions, symbols, and ritual structure that most appeal to you.

- Continue this process for each of the remaining seven Sabbats. Realize that you probably won't be able to do this in one night.

- Find, borrow, or write your own words for each Sabbat. Don't be hesitant to borrow or adapt printed invocations – it's an old Wiccan habit. Use extra pages if necessary. Work through the Sabbats in the same order, recording the words that you've chosen for each ritual occasion. Don't rush this; these words may very well become the heart of your Wiccan rites.

- Finally, 'marry' the elements that you've assembled for Yule into a presentable ritual. Write out your ritual. Include the symbols, the colors (if appropriate, for altar cloths, candles and etc.), the words and ritual actions. Repeat this process for the rest of the Sabbats.

- Fine-tune the rituals. Add 'Cast the circle' and any other ritual instructions that you've left out.

- Copy the rituals into your Book of Shadows – and be prepared to make further corrections or changes as you feel fit.

- Finally, during the next year, try your rituals on the appropriate dates.

Creating the Sabbat rituals is a challenging process that requires thought, research and time. The ultimate result, a set of workable Sabbat rituals specifically designed to meet your needs, is clearly worth the effort. Creating your own Sabbat rituals is a wonderful way to demonstrate your devotion to Wicca.

SABBAT	SYMBOLISM	RITUAL ACTIONS	SYMBOLS
Yule	Renewal and rebirth during Winter	Fires lit, candles carried around the circle; Yule log	Colors are green and red; wheel symbol, evergreens, Yule log, small potted tree
Imbolc	Festival of Lights	Candles lit and held in Circle, Blessing of seeds, wheel symbol placed on altar	Colors are white, green and white, or blue. Dish of snow; evergreens; candles
Ostara	The start of Spring	Fire is lit in Circle during (not before) rite itself	Color is white. Potted plant; cauldron or balefire
Beltane	The return of Fertility	Weaving ribbons, bonfire leaping, horn blowing	Color is white. Fresh flowers; cauldron filled with flowers; mirrors
Litha	Great, magical power	Flower-rimed cauldron, sword plunged into cauldron, bonfire leaping, herb-drying	Color is white. Mugwort; mirrors to capture the sun (or the flames of the fire)
Lughnasadh	Harvest and thanksgiving	Bread eaten and thrown into fire, grains woven into Goddess and God symbols	Colors are red and orange. Corn dollies; special loaves of bread; grain
Mabon	Second harvest and Mysteries	Fruit is honored; ritual sprinkling of leaves	Colors are red and brown. Pine cones; acorns; wheat; dried leaves
Samhain	The end of Summer; the Dead are honored	Scrying in smoke, candle flame, fire or mirror; calling departed ones; leave food outside after ritual	Colors are red or black. Pomegranates; pumpkins; apples

AFTERWORD

Following these guidelines to fashion your Esbat and Sabbat rituals will create basically Wiccan rituals. Breaking with such traditional patterns could, however, lead you into decidedly non-Wiccan territory.

Just as one bolt of cloth can be cut and stitched into a huge variety of objects, from pillow cases to teddy bears to clothing, so too can Wiccan ritual be fashioned in many ways. However, if you wish to make a shirt from that cloth but decide not to include sleeves, you won't end up with a shirt.

A new Wiccan tradition's rituals must also be carefully crafted, following established forms, to avoid sewing a shirt that can't be worn. Though Wiccan ritual structure is a bit loose, those aspects of it that are set must be followed if you're to continue practicing Wicca.

These words aren't meant to frighten you. Creating a new Wiccan tradition can be difficult. It requires attention to detail and a bit of imagination or creativity – but this creative thought must be placed within a Wiccan context.

If not, you'll simply be creating a new religion.

SUGGESTED READING

For background information regarding Esbats, see:

Valiente's *An ABC of Witchcraft*, pages 135-137.

Guiley's *The Encyclopedia of Witches and Witchcraft*, pages 113-114.

For actual Esbat and Full Moon ritual texts, see:

Valiente's *Witchcraft For Tomorrow*. (See pages 168-170)

Buckland's *The Complete Book of Witchcraft*. (Page 61-62)

Buckland's *The Tree*. (Pages 50-53)

Slater's *A Book of Pagan Rituals*. (The rite termed 'Pagan Ritual For General Use' on p. 8-10 is essentially an Esbat; pages 55-57 contain a Pagan solitary full moon rite. Please note: these aren't strictly Wiccan rituals.)

Cunningham, *Wicca: A Guide for the Solitary Practitioner*. (Pages 124-126)

For background information concerning the Sabbats, see:

Valiente's *An ABC of Witchcraft*. (Article headed "Yule", pp.406-408)

Farrar's *What Witches Do*. (Pages 95-107)

Farrar and Farrar's *Eight Sabbats for Witches* (Pages 61-150)

Guiley's *The Encyclopedia of Witches and Witchcraft*. (Pages 288-290).

Frazer's *The Golden Bough*. (Pages 705-763. Bear in mind that much of what Frazer discusses isn't performed by Wiccans. However, these words preserve proof of the ancient existence of the Pagan fire festivals that eventually evolved into what we know today as the Sabbats. This section of the book is virtually required reading for all Wiccans.)

Burland, *Echoes of Magic*. (The entire book is of great interest. Unfortunately, it's now impossible to find and was never printed in the U.S. Check libraries – that's where I found a copy.)

For actual Sabbat ritual scripts, see:

Starhawk, *The Spiral Dance*. (Pages 169-183 contain a full set of 8 Sabbat rites.)

Z Budapest, *The Holy Book of Women's Mysteries*. (The God isn't included.)

Farrar and Farrar, *Eight Sabbats for Witches*. (Pages 61-150)

Buckland, *The Tree: The Complete Book of Saxon Witchcraft*. (Pages 57-77 includes 8 complete Sabbat rites.)

Slater (editor), *A Book of Pagan Rituals*. (Written for non-initiates. Pages 23-42 nominally describe Wiccan group Sabbat rituals; here termed "The Eight Grove Festivals". Pages 58-79 include complete Solitary rituals, which is one of the reasons for this book's popularity. This isn't strictly Wiccan, but it's pretty close.)

Cunningham, Wicca: A Guide for the Solitary Practitioner. (This book's complement includes 8 Solitary Sabbat rites on pages 127-143.)

17: RITUAL DESIGN PART 2

Yes, there's more, but relax. This part's much easier than writing your Esbat and Sabbat rites. It consists of determining the shape of a few other, far less complicated rites.

THE CIRCLE

By this time you've probably found a suitable circle casting. If not, now's the time to decide. You should know which tools are used and how they're used. The readings offer many examples.

So much has been written about the circle casting itself that I feel that to rephrase it here would be meaningless. Therefore, I'll discuss other aspects below.

In actually determining the circle casting to use, you may adopt one that's appeared in a book, or utilize it as the basis to your own. In any case, the circle casting is an important ritual.

To be as brief as possible, here's a breakdown on the outer ritual steps that usually compose a circle casting:

- Purifying the area.

- Setting up the altar.

- Lighting the candles and incense.

- Consecrating the water.

- Blessing the salt.

- Actual magical creation of the circle.

- Sprinkling of salt around circle. Carrying of smoking censer around circle. Carrying of flaming candle around circle. Sprinkling of water around circle. (I stress that, while such a form is used by many Wiccans, it's hardly the only method of casting the circle.)

Besides knowing the outer mechanics of circle casting, you should also be well aware of the internal processes that occur within you during circle casting (including energy raising and releasing, visualizations and changes in consciousness). Once you've decided on one specific circle casting, become completely familiar with and comfortable with it. It's best if it can be memorized in its entirety.

It's also time to determine your tradition's basic concept of the circle. How strong is it? Can you walk through it, or do you have to cut a doorway to leave the circle? If so, how do you make a doorway? What about pets and children who roam into your circle? Will they harm it? Will it have to be recast when this occurs?

What's the circle's function? To keep energy in? To keep something else out? Both? Or it is simply a place that you create to meet with the Goddess and God? Is the circle necessary for every ritual, even those that occur outdoors? What about emergencies?

Determining this information will allow you to make stronger, more effective circles. Why? Because you'll know your circle forward and backward. You'll have no uncertainties regarding its purpose or function. (You'll also have to create your circle releasing rite. See the readings.)

TOOL CONSECRATION

Many traditions utilize a specific ritual for the consecration of tools. Some use the four elements (Earth, Air, Fire and Water) in such rituals. Others, a sprinkling of blessed salt and consecrated water. Some type of incantation should be created, borrowed or adapted which aptly sums up the ritual action. Such rites are usually quite short and rely far more on the consecrator's energy than on the ritual form itself.

CAKES AND WINE

Cakes and Wine (also known as Cakes and Ale and, in this book's successor, as The Simple Feast) is the rite-within-a-rite that both grounds energy and directly links us with the Goddess and God, since we're consuming food created on Their planet.

The ritual is quite simple: the cakes (cookies) and wine (juice) are blessed by a short prayer dedicated to the Goddess and God. A small portion may be left on the altar or in an offering bowl to be given later to the earth, and the food is eaten in ritual. Again, this is a short rite.

Many Wiccans use cookies that they've specially baked for the 'cakes'. Others use crackers or even store-brought cookies. Many Wiccans don't drink wine. If you do, which type is most appropriate for Cakes and Wine? If you don't drink wine, what's a good substitute? Grape juice? Apple juice?

Writing these rituals isn't as difficult as it may appear, especially if you adapt and borrow from other traditions. They're necessary in every Wiccan tradition and should be finalized for your new tradition.

There are other rites that you can write or adapt as you see fit. These aren't strictly necessary in what will probably be a Solitary Wiccan tradition, but you might wish to have them on hand and copy them into your

Book of Shadows – just in case. (For examples, see the readings listed at the end of this chapter.)

HANDFASTING
(A WICCAN MARRIAGE CEREMONY)

You may not need one, but then again, you just might. Such ceremonies, of course, aren't legally binding unless they're performed by a person so empowered by the state in which the people reside. This may or may not be of concern.

BIRTH CEREMONY

Some call these 'Wiccanings' but I dislike the term. You may have questions concerning this rite as well: is the baby being dedicated to the Goddess and God? If so, shouldn't she or he have a say in the matter? And, thus, should this be done at a later age? If the rite is purely protective and celebratory, in which the child is shown to the Goddess and God, such questions need not arise. It depends on the way you write the ritual.

DEATH CEREMONY

Wiccans as a group don't ritualize mourning. Death is a doorway through which souls pass to re-enter the realm of the Goddess. Bodies are simply suits that we wear and use until they wear out, or until we have no need for further lessons and opportunities in this lifetime. Bodies should be taken care of, but their deaths (the soul never dies) aren't, traditionally speaking, times for *ritualized* sorrow. How can it be in a religion that embraces reincarnation; that sees bodily death as but one of many such transitions that the human soul will experience?

Naturally, Wiccans grieve, and many have small rites to mark the transition of a loved one. Few of these rites have been printed. You may write your own if you feel the need.

SELF-INITIATION AND INITIATION RITUALS

Finally, you may wish to record your own self-initiation ceremony. You may even write or adapt an initiation ceremony, if you have any plans to ever teach others your Wiccan tradition. It's never too early to start planning.

SUGGESTED READING:

Circle Castings:
(Most of the below include both creating and releasing the circle.)

Farrar, *What Witches Do*. (Pages 56-60)

Valiente, *Witchcraft For Tomorrow*. (Pages 155-159)

Starhawk, *The Spiral Dance*. (Pages 55-57)

Cunningham, *Wicca: A Guide for the Solitary Practitioner*. (Pages 115-122)

Buckland, *The Tree*. (Pages 38-41; here entitled 'Erecting the Temple' and 'Clearing the Temple')

Consecration of Tools:
Farrar and Farrar, *The Witches' Way*. (Pages 44-48)

Cunningham, *Wicca: A Guide for the Solitary Practitioner*.

Slater, *Pagan Rituals III*. (Page 59)

Valiente's *Witchcraft For Tomorrow*. (Pages 164-166)

Cakes and Wine:
Farrar and Farrar, *Eight Sabbats for Witches*. (Page 46)

Slater, *Pagan Rituals III*. (Pages 69 and 70 contain blessings for the cakes and the wine.)

Buckland's *The Tree*. (Pages 54-56; here termed 'Cakes and Ale')

Buckland, *Buckland's Complete Book of Witchcraft*. (Page 63)

Cunningham's *Wicca: A Guide for the Solitary Practitioner*. (page 123; here termed the 'Simple Feast')

Handfastings:

Buckland, *Buckland's Complete Book of Witchcraft*. (Pages 97-99; includes, wisely, a Handparting as well.)

Buckland's *The Tree*. (Pages 78-81; a 'Hand-Parting' ceremony can be found on pp. 82-84.)

Farrar and Farrar, *Eight Sabbats for Witches*. (Pages 160-165)

Birth Celebrations:

Farrar and Farrar, *Eight Sabbats for Witches*. (Pages 153-159)

Buckland, *Buckland's Complete Book of Witchcraft*. (Pages 99-100)

Buckland's *The Tree: A Book of Saxon Witchcraft*. (Pages 85-87)

Death Ceremonies:

Farrar and Farrar, *Eight Sabbats for Witches*. (Pages 166-173; here termed 'Requiem'.)

Buckland, *The Tree*. (Pages 88-90; here termed 'Crossing the Bridge [At Death]'.)

Buckland, *Buckland's Complete Book of Witchcraft*. (Pages 100-101; termed as in the above entry.)

Self-Initiation:

Valiente's *Witchcraft For Tomorrow*. (Pages 159-164)

Farrar and Farrar, *The Witches' Way*. (Pages 244-250)

Initiations:

Farrar and Farrar, *The Witches' Way*. (Pages 9-20)

Buckland's Complete Book of Witchcraft. (Pages 46-49)

I've listed the above two sources because they're among the most complete treatments of initiation in print, but many, many other Wiccan books discuss initiation and/or provide ritual scripts. These are all for coven use, of course.

18: BELIEFS

'Beliefs' isn't the best word, but the only other ones that I could come up with were 'tenets' and 'concepts', neither of which is satisfactory. Since religion is usually conceived of as being built on beliefs, this word will have to serve.

GENERAL TRADITIONAL WICCAN BELIEFS

Aside from strictly deity-oriented beliefs, Wiccans share a few others, including:

- The Goddess and God are revered. This is central to Wiccan thought.

- Human souls enjoy a series of incarnations in human form. Reincarnation is one of the most wide-spread of Wiccan beliefs. Precisely how and why we incarnate several times is open to mystical speculation. Few Wiccan traditions have specific teachings regarding this doctrine. Some simply state that we reincarnate and meet others we've known in past lives. Others are more specific, some less specific. Some traditions say that we never switch sexes from one life to another; still others state that we choose whichever gender is appropriate for our evolutionary lessons. There's little agreement.

- Power can be sent in non-physical form to affect the world in positive ways. Thus, we accept both the practice of magic and its effectiveness.

- What is done will be returned to the doer. Precisely how this energy is returned has been a matter of great speculation. Some Wiccans state that the Goddess performs this function; others that it's a law of the universe, like gravity, and that no one being is in charge of seeing that this occurs. It's an automatic response, like a ricochet.

- The Earth is our home, our Goddess. It's not a tool that we can ruthlessly abuse. Ecological concerns are rather new in Wicca, but now play an important role. Many rituals are performed to give healing strength to the Earth. The ecological movement has had a tremendous impact on Wicca.

- Wiccans aren't evangelical. We have no need to go out and spread the word. Answering questions about our religion is far different from knocking on doors and asking strangers, "Have you heard the word of the Goddess today?" Such practices are certainly understandable (though irritating) in religions whose members believe that they've really found the only way, but are absurdly out of place in Wicca.

- Wicca accepts that every religion is correct to its adherents. This doesn't mean that we like every representative of every religion, but ecumenicism must be the way of life. Not only must we all tolerate each other, Wiccans will, in the future, share more dialogue with representatives of other religions to increase their knowledge of our ways. This is already occurring to a limited degree.

○ Wicca accepts members from both sexes, from every race, national origin and, usually, of every sexual preference. Unfortunately, racism and prejudice does exist in Wicca: many covens simply won't let non-Caucasians receive training and initiation. Such racism is usually covert and is rarely openly stated, but it does exist. Though Wiccans are human, and we've been taught from birth to like certain groups and to dislike others, we must overcome such idiotic concepts and realize that we're all people. Racism and prejudice in any form is anti-Wiccan. (Besides, who ever said that the Goddess is Caucasian?)

○ Wicca is a religion, not a political organization. Groups of Wiccan can and sometimes do work toward a common cause, and individual Wiccans may indeed become personally involved in the political system, but Wicca as a whole isn't a religion that preaches issues or supports specific political candidates. Some issues in which individual Wiccans have become involved include women's rights; reproductive freedom; land conservation; animal rights; restrictive religious legislation and other issues.* However, Wicca isn't a political religion. Some covens, in fact, ban discussion of politics before, during and after circle.

○ Wicca doesn't charge for private lessons or for initiation. Physical objects created by Wiccans (pentacles, knives, wands, incenses, oils, books) and services (such as public classes and Wiccan-based

---

*A good summary of a national example of individual Wiccan involvement in politics can be found in the article concerning the Helms Amendment (which would have removed tax-exempt status for religious Witchcraft and Neo-Pagan groups) in Rosemary Guiley's The Encyclopedia of Witches and Witchcraft, p. 156.

counseling) can and should be paid for, but not personal, private Wiccan instruction or initiation. In some groups, coven funds are kept to pay for ritual supplies; this is the only exception.

Virtually all Wiccans subscribe to the above list of beliefs. Certainly most traditions do. It's impossible to discover precisely how every individual Wiccan interprets these beliefs, but we can be assured that most of them do in one form or another.

It could be valuable for you to make a list of your personal Wiccan beliefs. Not just the raw beliefs themselves, but your interpretations of them. For example, you may write the following:

REINCARNATION

- We incarnate many times to learn our lessons.

- We may incarnate with people we've known in other lives.

- Cats reincarnate too.

What's important is to bring your beliefs to paper. This crystallizes them; firms them. Beliefs can become rather hazy. Such an exercise can define them.

Your interpretations of the general Wiccan beliefs may and probably will change as you grow in experience and understanding. This is natural. The list that you've made may become out of date. This, too is fine.

Wicca is a religion that teaches specific beliefs. We should be fully familiar with them if we're to practice this religion. It may take time for you to completely accept some of these beliefs. Study, think, pray and experiment.

Wiccan beliefs are the heart of Wicca.

19: RULES

Virtually all religious organizations give their adherents a set of guide-lines or rules of conduct. In such laws we often find the true nature of the faith, which can be difficult to determine from the actual behavior of most of its representatives.

Wicca possesses not one but several sets of such rules. The most famous of these, which has been published in several different forms, originally stemmed from what is now known as Gardnerian Wicca.[*]

Many other versions exist, and some covens create their own set of laws for use by its members. Underlying all such Wiccan rules is one basic concept: Harm none.

Traditional Wiccan laws can be grouped into specific categories for study. Looking at these, and reading a few sample sets (included at the end of this chapter), should readily provide all that you need to write or adapt a set of laws for your tradition.

Here's a basic breakdown of traditional Wiccan laws. The first section details laws specifically concerned with coven working, which are of less importance to Solitary Wiccans. The second section is devoted to laws of great potential use to the Solitary practitioner.

For a fascinating look at the possible origins of these laws, see Witchcraft For Tomorrow *by Doreen Valiente.*

TRADITIONAL WICCAN LAWS — COVEN ORIENTED

COVEN HEIRARCHY/ORGANIZATION

Usually lists duties of High Priestess and High Priest. The average length of time that the 'offices' are held is also often discussed. Many delineate initiatory levels and define the nature of the 'council of elders' (usually made of those who have received the highest elevation, and who are called upon for guidance and counsel by coven members), or other such groups within the group. Many also describe other coven officers.

SECRECY

Traditional warnings to keep secret those things which are only for the eyes and ears of other initiates of the same tradition. Some laws threaten the oath-breaker with divine retribution if the oaths are broken. (Solitary Wiccans can certainly create a 'secret' tradition. Whether you care to discuss your religion and your religious practices with others must be a personal decision. Only you can decide precisely what to reveal.)

COVEN PROBLEMS

Dictates the proper method of settling problems. Some covens utilize their 'council of elders' in the decision-making process, or to provide guidance to those with grievances. In most traditions, the highest-elevated Wiccans are free to leave and form their own covens, if they can no longer work with their parent coven. Many laws also concern High Priestesses and High Priests who break the laws or who lose interest in the coven.

PERSECUTION TALES AND ADVICE

These supposedly ancient laws allow for confession during extreme torture, but thoughtfully permits denial of all information given to the 'magistrates'. It also contains the promise that drugs will reach those who have been condemned as Witches so that their certain deaths by execution will be less painful. (This is obviously of little help today.)

RITUAL ATTENDANCE

Many traditions possess laws regarding attendance at rituals. Great latitude exists, and not all traditions even have such laws. In most, Wiccans are expected to show up for all rituals unless previously excused by the coven leader(s). In some sets of rules, missing six consecutive meetings is grounds for 'banishment' from the coven, if only because the Wiccan is showing little or no interest. (This is of little concern to Solitaries. However, a few words of encouragement concerning the regular observance of our rituals would be a nice touch to include in your set of laws.)

TRADITIONAL LAWS OF INTEREST
TO SOLITARY WICCANS

WORSHIP

Sometimes lists times and dates of ritual observances; more generally, the laws state that the Goddess and God are deserving of worship, and remind the Wiccans to be worshipful. (This makes sense. Why else would we be Wiccans? Such words might appear in the beginning of the law.)

BLOODSHED

Many laws state that blood is not to be shed within the circle; no ritual animal sacrifices may be made. (This is a universal Wiccan tradition, whether or not it's explicitly stated in the laws.)

AVOIDANCE OF HARM

The central, unifying theme of most laws: Wiccans simply don't cause harm to others. (This law, in some form or another, should be in your set.)

USE OF MAGIC

Generally states that magic is not to be worked for pay, as it could lead to performing destructive rites. Magic is also never to be used to boost one's pride or to cause harm in any way. However, some sets of laws do allow Wiccans to use 'the power' (i.e., magic) to 'prevent or restrain' others from causing harm (this is generally known as binding). (See "'The Law of the Power' below.)

CONDUCT

Such laws warn Wiccans not to boast or to threaten others, and to treat others – Wiccans and non-Wiccans – with kindness and compassion. Additionally, some laws state that Wiccans must not use drugs within or without the circle; must not gossip about other members, and mustn't interfere with the teachings of other Wiccans .(It never hurts to include such messages in your laws. Though you may be the only one to read these reminders of the importance of kindness, the message may, at times, be necessary.)

TEACHING

Some laws state that all who express interest in Wicca should be taught, unless they begin to misuse their instructions. Such laws have largely been either dropped or reinterpreted. Truly following them today could lead to each Wiccan teaching 100 or more students, which would result in poor lessons and, thus, poorly-instructed students. Such laws simply aren't practical in today's world when so many clamor for teachings.

KEEPING THE LAW

Wiccans are reminded to keep the law and not to allow it to be broken. (Sound advice. This usually appears near the end of the laws.)

THE LOVE OF THE GODDESS AND THE GOD

A gentle reminder that we're not alone. (Generally, it's best to begin and to end the law with confirmations of divine concern.)

❂   ❂   ❂

After reading all this, you might be thinking, "Why do I even need a Law if I'm just doing my rituals alone?" A fair question, even if we set aside those laws concerning covens.

The answer is simple; most of the laws appropriate to Solitary Wiccans form part of the general Wiccan tradition. Without them, we are left without guidance. Forming them into set sentences and including them in your tradition's Book of Shadows ensures that you can study them at your leisure, and refer to them for guidance.

It's all very well to state, "I won't do this, and I'll remember to do that." Having a set of laws concerning these things is a great memory assistant.

SAMPLE LAWS

Using the above outlines of laws, we can come up with our own. Their precise form, and their method of presentation, is completely up to you. Some sets of laws are numbered; others aren't. Some are written in rhyming couplets, but most are in prose.

Here are three versions, that I've written. The first is partially based on the above analyses; the second is reprinted from *Wicca: A Guide for the Solitary Practitioner*, as is the third, which deals exclusively with magic.

THE LAW

- We are of the Old Ways, among those who walk with the Goddess and God and receive Their love.

- Keep the Sabbats and Esbats to the best of your abilities, for to do otherwise is to lessen your connections with the Goddess and God.

- Harm none. This, the oldest law, is not open to interpretation or change.

- Shed not blood in ritual; the Goddess and God need not blood to be duly worshipped.

- Those of our way are kind to all creatures, for hurtful thoughts are quite draining and aren't worth the loss of energy. Misery is self-created; so, too, is joy, so create joy and disdain misery and unhappiness. And this is within your power. So harm not.

- Teach only what you know, to the best of your ability, to those students whom you choose, but teach not to those who would use your instructions for destruction or control. Also, teach not to boost pride, for ever remember: she who teaches for vain-glory shall take little pride in her handiwork; she who teaches out of love shall be enfolded in the arms of the Goddess and God.

○ Ever remember that if you would be of our way, keep the Law close to your heart, for it is the nature of the Wicca to keep the Law.

○ If ever the need arises, any law may be changed or discarded, and new laws written to replace them, so long as the new laws don't break the oldest law of all: harm none.

○ Blessings of the God and Goddess on us all.

THE NATURE OF OUR WAY

○ As often as possible, hold the rites in forests, by the seashore, on deserted mountain tops or near tranquil lakes. If this is impossible a garden or some chamber shall suffice, if it is readied with fumes or flowers.

○ Seek out wisdom in books, rare manuscripts and cryptic poems if you will, but seek it out also in simple stones and fragile herbs and in the cries of wild birds. Listen to the whisperings of the wind and the roar of water if you would discover magic, for it is here that the old secrets are preserved.

○ Books contain words; trees contain energies and wisdom books ne'er dreamt of.

○ Ever remember that the Old Ways are constantly revealing them-selves. Therefore be as the river willow that bends and sways with the wind. That which remains changeless shall outlive its spirit, but that which evolves and grows will shine for centuries.

○ Mock not the rituals or spells of another, for who can say yours are greater in power or wisdom?

○ Ensure that your actions are honorable, for all that you do shall return to you three-fold, good or bane.

○ Be wary of one who would dominate you, who would control and manipulate your workings and reverences. True reverence for the Goddess and God occurs within. Look with suspicion on any who would twist worship from you for their own gain and glory, but welcome those priestesses and priests who are suffused with love.

○ Honor all living things, for we are of the bird, the fish, the bee Destroy not life save it be to preserve your own.

○ And this is the nature of our way.

THE LAW OF THE POWER

○ The Power shall not be used to bring harm, to injure or control others. But if the need arises, the Power shall be used to protect your life or the lives of others.

○ The Power is used only as need dictates.

○ The Power can be used for your own gain, as long as by doing so you harm none.

○ It is unwise to accept money for use of the Power, for it quickly controls its taker. Be not as those of other religions.

○ Use not the Power for prideful gain, for such cheapens the mysteries of Wicca and magic.

- Ever remember that the Power is the sacred gift of the Goddess and God, and should never be misused or abused.

- And this is the Law of the Power.

Most Craft laws are secret, and can't be published in any form. However, the above examples included in this chapter, and in the suggested readings, should provide you with enough information to create your own laws.

May you do so with wisdom and love.

SUGGESTED READINGS

Published laws

Few sets of Wiccan laws have been published. Even most of the standard Wiccan guidebooks fall to include laws.

However, a few books do include discussions of and/or complete texts of laws. Here are most of them. Studying these laws in concert with this chapter will greatly assist in the creation of your own set. (For additional publication information regarding these books, see this book's Bibliography.)

Kelly, Aidan A., *Crafting the Art of Magic, Book 1*. Contains one version of the 'Gardnerian' laws on pp. 145-161. Also includes an intriguing 'Proposed Rules for the Craft' on pp. 103-105.

See also Doreen Valiente's *The Rebirth of Witchcraft*, pp. 69-71 for background information concerning both the "Proposed Rules" as well as the Gardnerian laws. The whole inside story concerning the most famous set of Wiccan laws is quite fascinating.

Additional information concerning these laws – without the text itself – can be discovered on pp. 303-304 of Janet and Stewart Farrar's *The Witches Way*.

Johns, June, *King of The Witches*. Contains another version of the Gardnerian laws in Appendix A, where they're mislabeled as 'The Book of Shadows'.

Slater, Heron (editor), *Pagan Rituals III, Outer Court Book of Shadows*. Originally written by the late Ed Buczynski for students of his Welsh tradition, this book contains a rather forceful section entitled 'The Laws' on pp.113-115. Though short, it's a good guide to some tradition's secret (non-Gardnerian) laws, though many are far gentler.

(Keep in mind that this was written for students, not for experienced Wiccans.)

Various other sets of Wiccan laws have been published in old pagan periodicals, most notably in the earlier format of *Green Egg*. The issues that contain these laws are now out of print and are, thus, avidly sought by collectors. (Some of these laws, by the way, have been added to 'traditional' Books of Shadows with no hint as to their origination.)

20: WICCAN SYMBOLS

Symbols are an important part of many Wiccan traditions. They're used as magical shorthand in the Book of Shadows; as a graphic representation of Wicca or a specific Wiccan tradition (on correspondence, perhaps) and to empower magical tools and jewelry.

The first ritual symbols used in Wicca stemmed largely from ceremonial magic (particularly those found in *The Key of Solomon*; see Bibliography) and alchemy. Their number soon increased and became more specifically Wiccan, such as symbols for levels of initiation, the circle, the Goddess and the God. Traditions shared symbols among their adherents. They began to be published, further widening their usage.

Your tradition should probably utilize some symbols. Symbols (which are, in a sense, a compact alphabet) trigger powerful psychological responses, if their observer is aware of their meanings, because they speak to the subconscious mind.

You can create your own symbols or choose ones from those lists given below. I have only one warning: never use an unfamiliar symbol. If you don't know a symbol's meaning, it's best not to utilize it in any way.

Here are some specific types of symbols:

SYMBOLS OF OUR RELIGION

The most famous of these is the pentagram, an interlaced five-pointed star. With one point upward, it represents Wicca. The pentagram's connection with our religion seems to be fairly modern (though the symbol itself has been in use since at least 2,400 B.C.E., when it appeared on Middle Eastern pottery).

Other symbols include small representations (usually in jewelry form) of goddesses, particularly the so-called 'Venus' statuettes such as the famous Venus of Willendorf.

(One recent symbol of Wicca was a plain green button, without lettering or signs, that was worn by Wiccans in public places so that they could greet each other. The practice has, as far as I know, died out on a national basis.)

TRADITION SYMBOLS

Many Wiccan Traditions use a specific symbol. Though it may be of any design, most include one or more of the following parts, which can be arranged in a number of unusual and striking ways:

Pentagram

Ankh

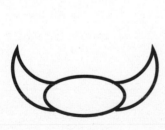

Crescent Moon

Horns

Eight-pointed Star

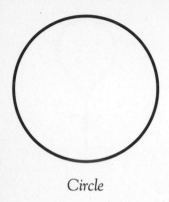

Circle

Yonic Symbols
(*particularly popular with some
feminist Wiccans*)

As can be seen from the illustrations, there are many potential combinations of these elements.

Such a symbol need not be created for your tradition. However, if you do design one, it can be copied into the Book of Shadows; stitched onto robes; painted onto tools and otherwise used in ritual ways.

BOOK OF SHADOWS SYMBOLS AND SHORTHAND

Following are some symbols used in various Wiccan traditions, with a few variations and quite a few of my own. Once you're comfortable with them, using them in writing rituals or in the Book of Shadows is quite convenient. For example, it's much easier to write "Cast O" than it is to write "Cast the magic circle."

Here are some traditional (and new) symbols:

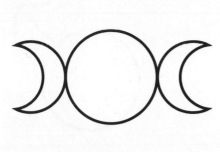

Goddess

God

Magic Circle

Goddess Position
*(a body posture sometimes used
in Wiccan ritual the Wiccan
stands with legs spread and holds
her arms out to her sides to
represent the Goddess)*

God Position
*(sometimes used in Wiccan
ritual; the Wiccan stands with
legs firmly together and wrists
crossed on his chest, usually right
over left, to represent the God)*

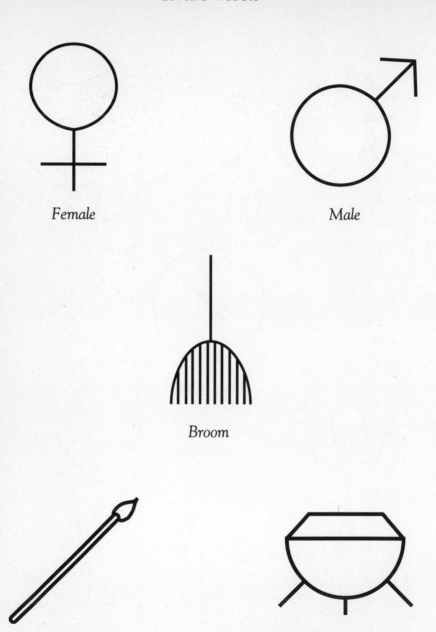

Female

Male

Broom

Wand

Cauldron

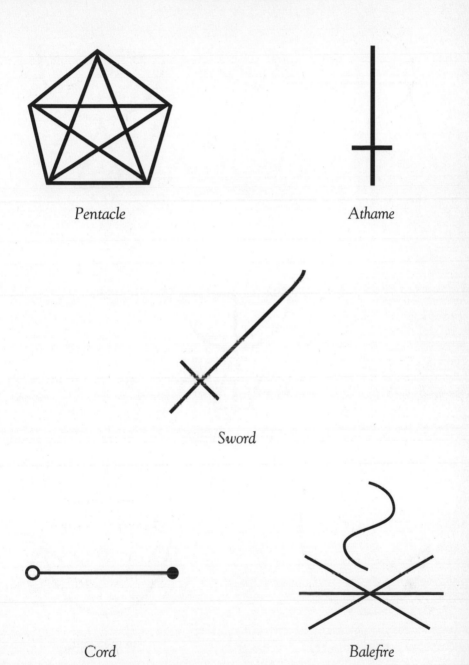

Pentacle

Athame

Sword

Cord

Balefire

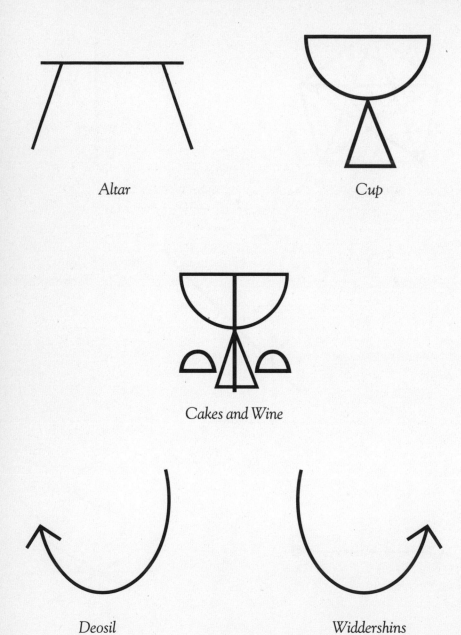

Altar

Cup

Cakes and Wine

Deosil

Widdershins

Maiden

Mother

Crone

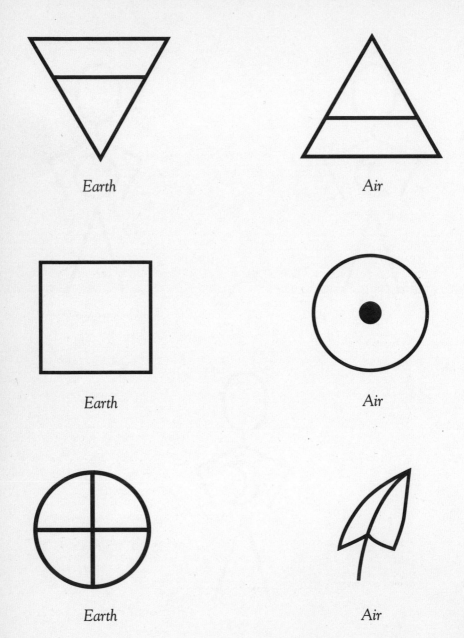

Earth

Air

Earth

Air

Earth

Air

Fire

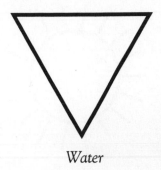

Water

Fire

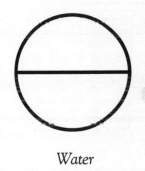

Water

Fire

Water

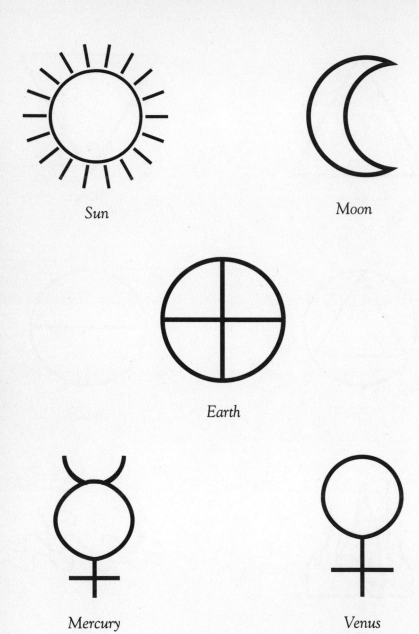

Sun

Moon

Earth

Mercury

Venus

Mars

Jupiter

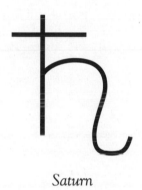

Saturn

Uranus

Neptune

New Moon

Waxing Moon

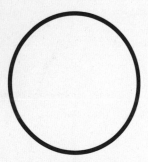

Full Moon

Waning Moon

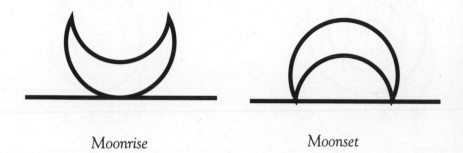

Moonrise   Moonset

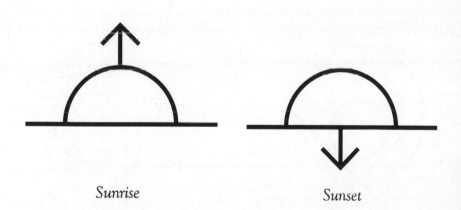

Sunrise   Sunset

Rebirth

Purification

Spell

Bane; Deadly

Blessings

Spirituality

Spirituality

Peace

Protection

Protection

Healing & Health

Courage

Magical Energy

Physical & Magical Strength

Beauty

Love

Love

Marriage

Friendship

Love

Psychic Awareness

Psychic Awareness

Conscious Mind

Money

Money

Rain

Storm

Sex

Fertility

Essential Oil

Plant
(herbs, flowers, leaves)

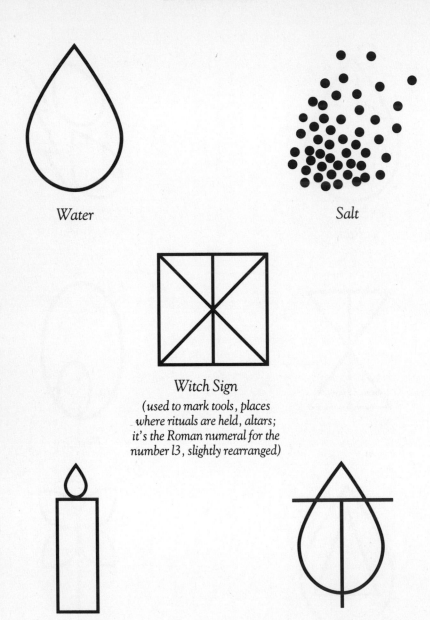

Water

Salt

Witch Sign
*(used to mark tools, places
where rituals are held, altars;
it's the Roman numeral for the
number 13, slightly rearranged)*

Candle

Wine

Spring

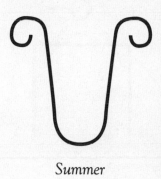

Summer

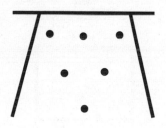

Winter

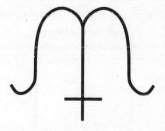

Autumn

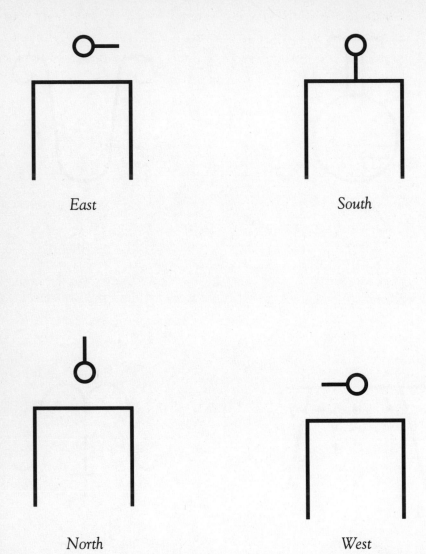

East

South

North

West

Use the above symbols to create your own rituals. You can tailor your spells to your specific need. The following are a few of my own. Refer to Chapter 19 of *Earth, Air, Fire & Water* (Llewellyn Publications) for more information on creating your own rituals.

To Cause Sleep

To Have Psychic Dreams

To Remember Dreams

To Prevent Drowsiness

For Studying

To Release Jealousy

To Release Guilt

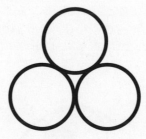

To Reduce Stress

To Quit Smoking

To Lose Weight

To Succeed in Business

To Excel in Interviews

To Gain Employment

Travel

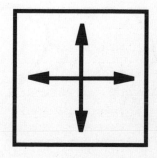

Protection During Traveling

To Protect 1 Child

To Protect 2 Children

To Protect 3 Children

To Strengthen Marriage

PERSONAL WICCAN SYMBOLS

Many Wiccans place a special symbol next to their signature as a sign of their religion and also, sometimes, for protective reasons. In some traditions, the symbol signifies the initiatory degree that she or he has reached.

I usually place a pentagram near my signature. You may use this or create your own symbol. It might be connected with the Goddess or God; it may be something entirely personal and unique. Call upon your imagination and creativity.

RUNIC ALPHABETS

Some Wiccans write their rituals in runes. Many don't, for complete familiarity with runes is necessary before they can be read at will, and few persons today are willing to learn a new alphabet. Still, most Wiccan traditions include a runic alphabet in their Books of Shadows.

Why? Runes may be used in specific magical rites for their symbolism and their inherent power. Additionally, runes are often painted or carved onto tools to enhance their effectiveness. Besides, it's traditional for Wiccans to use runes in one way or another.

Many runic alphabets have been published. (At one time, while these were still considered to be secret, entire runic alphabets could be found in many dictionaries). Today, the wide range of books available on this subject allows us to choose the system best-suited to our purposes.

There's so much disagreement concerning the precise form of runic alphabets (let alone their meanings) that I won't add to it here by including yet another variation. I suggest, if you're interested, to read the books listed below.

SUGGESTED READING

Howard, Michael, *The Magic of Runes*. (The entire book)

Koch, Rudolf, *The Book of Signs*. (The entire book)

Tyson, Donald, *Rune Magic*. (The entire book)

21: THE BOOK OF SHADOWS

Most Wiccan traditions treasure a Book of Shadows. Such books are rarely published or even shown to non-initiates. In them, the tradition's specific beliefs and modes of worship are thoroughly or sketchily outlined.

Though contents and organization of these ritual manners vary, most Books of Shadows include instructions for the circle casting and banishing; religious rituals; the consecration of tools; laws; coven organizational notes; magical rites; prayers and perhaps herbal lore. Some contain lists of the tradition's pantheon, training exercises for new students and, finally, initiation ceremonies.

Such books are vitally important to the establishment and maintenance of all Wiccan traditions, for without them, the tradition's specific rites and other lore must be carefully memorized and passed down by word of mouth. This always leaves room for error, misinterpretation, and even loss of the material.

Don't misunderstand this: no Wiccan tradition that I know of has recorded every single bit of information. Much is verbally passed from teacher to student. Still, a tradition's Book of Shadows provides an unchanging guide and memory-trigger for the practitioner.

There are many different Books of Shadows today. Some are used by hundreds or thousands of Wiccans. Others are created by Solitary Wiccans and are never shown to others.

This chapter is a guide to writing your own Book of Shadows. In a sense, it's the culmination of Part III of this book – for it's in this book that you'll record your new tradition.

The book itself can be of any type. Bound blank books are widely available today and can certainly be used – but only if you're sure that your tradition has stopped evolving. (It's difficult to make changes in a bound book.) If you have any doubt whatsoever, a loose-leaf notebook might be the answer. This allows you to add or delete new materials if and when the need arises.

Many traditional Wiccan Books of Shadows begin with initiation rituals, and contain other information that isn't directly applicable to Solitary Wiccans. If we set aside these sections, we can view the general (very general) outline of a typical Book of Shadows. This can be used when creating your own.

The process is simple; fill in the blanks with all the information, rituals, rules and other information that you've determined are a part of your tradition. Add your own touches – a bit of poetry here, maybe a section of songs or chants. Most Solitary Books of Shadows are highly personal creations.

(If you feel uncomfortable thinking about creating your own Book of Shadows, don't. Every Book of Shadows was written at sometime or another.)

- ✪ *Title Page*. This may say 'Book of Shadows', 'The Book of Shadows', or something more specific to your tradition, such as 'The Night Moon Tradition Book of Shadows' (if you've come up with a name for it). Alternately, the title page may bear only a pentagram, your name in runes, or other symbols. It can also be blank.

- *Laws.* These could also be termed 'Rules', 'codes' or 'Codes of conduct'.

- *Invocations of the Goddess and God* may appear next, or before the laws. One or two invocations often appear early in the book to 'bless' it.

- An *altar diagram*.

- *Circle casting and dispersing instructions.* Be as specific as possible.

- *Rituals:* Sabbats, Full Moon rite, tool consecrations, Cakes and Wine.

- *Prayers, chants and invocations* (for use as you see fit).

- *The Tools of the Craft.* (This can be placed in other locations. In some traditions, this information forms part of the initiation rites.)

- *Self-Initiation ritual.* And, if you desire, a coven initiation ritual. All other rituals of all kinds.

- *Magical rites and information,* including herbal lore and recipes as well as specifically Wiccan spells (i.e., those that directly involve the Goddess and God). Also, symbols and signs used in magical shorthand (in the Book of Shadows) as well as for magical purposes. Runes.

This sketchy outline can be altered to your liking.

Do you have to hand-write your Book of Shadows? Traditional Wiccans might say yes, but today many are typed or stored on disk and photocopied. still, there's no doubt that hand-writing every single word does enhance the effectiveness of the Book of Shadows, for a part of your energy then physically exists within the words and the book itself.

If you have terrible handwriting, or simply don't like to write, you can either type it or key it into a computer and print it out.

Though computing your Book of Shadows may seem to be quite convenient, nothing is more evocative than turning to a hand-written book during ritual. It's part of the romantic legacy of Wicca, and one we shouldn't be without. (I would agree, however, due to recent personal experience, that a typed copy of everything hand-written can come in handy. In other words, the Book of Shadows in both forms may well be the ideal.)

SUGGESTED READING

Many alleged Books of Shadows have seen print, in varying formats. They're in more or less complete versions, but many have been highly altered for publication by their presenters. Here are a few of them, with notes regarding each:

Valiente, 'The Liber Umbrarum' in *Witchcraft For Tomorrow*. (Written specifically for the Solitary Wiccan, this work unfortunately lacks Sabbat rituals.)

Buckland, *The Tree: A Book of Saxon Witchcraft*. (A new Wiccan tradition based on a Saxon cultural framework, but clearly Wiccan through and through.)

Farrar and Farrar, *The Witches' Way*. (Bits and pieces of the Gardnerian Book of Shadows and rituals; nothing complete. Chapters IV and V are of especial interest.)

Slater (editor), *A Book of Pagan Rituals* (Pagan-Way public materials, not quite Wiccan.)

Slater (editor), *Pagan Rituals III: Outer Court Training Coven*. (The second half of this work, 'Book of Mysteries' is a fairly complete coven-based Book of Shadows written for students of a Welsh tradition.)

Weinstein, *Earth Magic: A Dianic Book of Shadows*. (Perhaps the most singular of these works; an unusual guide to some aspects of Wiccan religious workings. No Sabbat rituals are included.)

Starhawk, *The Spiral Dance*. (A Book of Shadows is scattered throughout this book.)

Reading just three or four of these published Books of Shadows may cause some confusion, but you'll quickly grasp the concept of Wicca's great variety. Remember: just because one Book of Shadows says that Wiccans do such-and-such is no reason why you must do so as well.

If you wish to create your own Wiccan tradition, it should possess a Book of Shadows. Though it can (and probably will) evolve over time, your Book of Shadows will stand as a symbol of your personal involvement with our religion; as a reaffirmation of your Wiccanhood.

And please, no matter how much you may dislike it, consider hand-copying your Book of Shadows. Think of it as an act of dedication to your religion.

22: TEACHING
(WIDENING THE CIRCLE)

Y ou already know more about Wicca than many others. You may not be an expert, and you probably have many questions, but others who've never read a book or performed a Wiccan ritual have even more questions. As you continue to practice, read and reflect on your Wiccan activities, your knowledge and experience will grow. If you mention your religion to even a few other persons, chances are that, eventually, someone will ask you to teach her or him because, after all, you're an expert.

This may not occur, but if it does you have an important decision before you: to teach or not to teach. Answering the below questions may assist you in making this decision.

Do I have the necessary knowledge and experience?
In other words, are you proficient at basic Wiccan ritual skills; familiar with the tools; have a good understanding of the Sabbats, and enjoy a deep relationship with the Goddess and God? Even if you aren't an expert at coven-oriented Wicca, are you an expert in your own form?

Do I have the skills to teach others?
Can you explain complex theories in simple language? Are you skilled at actually demonstrating Wiccan techniques to a student? You needn't have chalkboard and ruler to be a teacher. There are many forms of teaching. The best of these, when teaching Solitary Wicca, is a mixture of honest talk and ritual demonstration (nothing heavy).

Do I have unlimited patience?

Can you repeat an answer to a question many times? Are you easily frustrated, especially with other humans? Do you believe that there are 'dumb questions'? Do you mind an occasional phone call at 2 AM?

Do I know how to pick a student?

This is an important question. Potential students are of every kind of human. If someone studies for a few months and then never calls again, you haven't wasted much time, and you may indeed have had a positive impact upon that person's life. If you teach someone who's unable to accept 'harm none' and goes on to utilize Wiccan magical techniques in harmful ways, you may feel guilty at your choice of students. If you teach a man or woman simply because you're involved with her or him, you may well be wasting your breath. Friends are another iffy proposition, for an established friendship doesn't guarantee a suitable student.

Do I really want to teach?

Are you pleased with the idea of revealing a very personal aspect of your life to others? Do you wish to assume the responsibility of teaching?

If so, why?

What are your true motivations? Glory? Worship from your student? Ego-strokes? Or the need to assist other humans with their spiritual development and happiness? Do you have an unconscious desire to 'spread the word' of Wicca (a taboo), or do you simply wish to fulfill a need that has expressed itself?

How much time are you willing to invest in classes?

Even if you have only one student, you may wish to prepare notes for upcoming classes; read up on different aspects so that you'll be fresh; find ways of communicating difficult Wiccan subjects in a way that they're comprehensible to your student; block out time for classes and/or rituals, and other time-consuming projects. The number of classes that you teach is up to you – once a week seems to be about right.

How much can your student afford to spend?

Though there's no fee for private Wiccan instruction, there are supplies that have to be purchased: tools, books, candles, incense. If your student has a tight budget, are you willing to loan books and tools to your student, or purchase duplicate supplies for their use? (Warning: most loaned Wiccan books are never returned.)

Your answers to these questions may well assist you in making the decision. If you decide that you're simply not ready, or don't want to begin teaching, explain this to the person who asked for instruction. If you do decide to teach others, it's time to begin planning your classes.

The format of such lessons, as well as their length and frequency, are entirely in your hands. Classes on a specific day of the week (or month) are a good idea, since this helps the student to remember the date.

Generally, it's best to teach in your own home. This way, when a question arises, you'll be able to show the student precisely what you've been talking about (in a book, with an illustration or using a tool that you may not have with you at the student's house).

Classes are best held in private, though not necessarily in secret. Trying to explain the casting of a circle while three small children run underfoot, turn on the television, and let the dogs and cats into the living room will result in a wasted lesson. Ensure that you and your student will be alone together.

Here are some more suggested guidelines for teaching:

Teach what you know.

This may seem obvious, but many persons try to pass on knowledge that they've barely grasped themselves. If you're no expert in certain subjects, don't pretend to teach them. If these topics come up in class, make a short explanation and continue; don't make them the focus of the class. *Teach with honesty.* When you don't know the answer to a question, simply say so, and perhaps you and your student can discover the answer together.

Don't let teaching rule your life.

It can be one aspect of it, and an important, fulfilling aspect, but it shouldn't become the sole purpose of your existence.

Teach with humor.

Forget the method in which you may have been taught the religion of your childhood. Wicca is far from a stern, forbidding religion. It's a religion of joy and love and pleasure, and your classes should reflect the nature of our way. If you're no stand-up comic, at least teach Wicca in a light-hearted way. No solemn warnings; no stern lectures.

Teach with humility.

Pomposity may temporarily impress the wide-eyed student, but extravagant claims concerning your power and wisdom can be quickly disproved even by the newest of students. Additionally, don't make your version of Wicca seem carved in stone. Remind your student that this is simply the way that you do things, and that there are many other ways. Don't constantly warn the student of the 'dangers' that may befall her or him after a skipped word in ritual. Such superstitious teachings have no place in Wicca.

Don't teach the ancient history of Wicca unless you're sure that it really exists.

Most books on this subject can't be trusted – even those written by Wiccans. If you wish, teach the modern history of Wicca, beginning with Gerald Gardner. We can at least be sure of the last 40 or so years.

Teach with common sense.

Don't have your student jump into the deep end the first few times out. Start small and increase the scope and complexity of your lessons. Ask your students if they've understood particularly important points, and be certain that they have before continuing on to more challenging topics. (You can always test them.)

Don't think of these classes as something to be endured.

Don't continue to teach a person who shows little interest in the subject, or who hints that she or he is practicing destructive magic.

Don't teach folk magic (see Glossary) as Wicca.

We all know that Wicca doesn't consist of spell casting and candle magic. Keep such distinctly non-religious, non-Wiccan practices limited to separate classes if you decide to teach them.

Don't teach to gain control over others.

This may seem to be another obvious warning, but some truly feel the need to dominate other persons. Since religion has been a dominant force in cultures throughout history, some begin teaching Wicca in order to become an authority figure. This, along with financial gain, are two of the worst reason for teaching.

Teach with love.

You may not love your student, but you should certainly love your religion. Let your feelings for Wicca show in your classes, but beware becoming a proselytizing, frothing, ranting fanatic in front of your students. Balance is recommended.

Never forget that you've made this decision to teach.

No one can truly force you to do anything. You've widened your circle and invited another to join it. Celebrate this fact.

Some sticky situations can arise when teaching, but all can be handled. After some training, or perhaps even before, your student may begin hinting around about initiation. This hinting may become more direct and open as time passes.

Never let such requests pass by without comment. Never give students false hope. If you don't wish to perform an initiation ritual upon another human being, tell your student this on the first day of class. Suggest self-initiation and, if you wish, describe your own rite. Make this perfectly clear. Some students will still harbor a faint hope, but at least you've set the record straight from the onset.

If you don't mind initiating others but don't yet know if the student is worthy, say that they'll have to pass a test after completing instruction before the possibility would even arise. And if you're already sure of the student's sincerity, simply say, "When the time is right." (Such initiation ceremonies aren't necessarily the culmination of private Wiccan teachings. In fact, they're rather rare. Still, every student wants an initiation. As a teacher, you'll have to deal with this.)

Another situation may arise. You'll most probably demonstrate a few rituals to your student. And eventually, your student will do ritual with you. This may lead to the false notion that you've formed a coven.

Once again, explain from the beginning that you're not forming a coven; you're not looking for other members, and the rituals will last only as long as the classes. (Students who have completely accepted the coven organization of Wicca often find it hard to let it go. This will come up in their attitudes.)

There's much more to be said regarding teaching, but you'll discover it as you go along. Since we're Solitary Wiccans, it certainly isn't necessary to teach others. However, it can be an especially rewarding activity on many levels.

Widening the circle is both a commitment to your religion and a celebration of your faith. It's also an endless learning experience. As I've always said, if you want to learn something, teach it.

23: LIVING WICCA

I titled this book *Living Wicca* for two reasons. First, Wicca is indeed living. It's thrived and grown in both popularity as well as in stature. The name of our religion is more frequently met with in the outside world, and sometimes in the most unexpected of places. Public awareness – and even a bit more understanding – is also growing. (The trend against public use of the terms 'Witchcraft' and 'Witch' has been a tremendous help to this process.)

This book's title also refers to its practitioners. We strive to live Wiccan lives, just as members of other religions attempt to fit their religious beliefs into their existences. Naturally, none of us is SuperWiccan; we all have to make difficult choices as the outside world intrudes into our lives. Some of these choices may well fly in the face of Wiccan teachings. Still, making the attempt to live a Wiccan life is certainly worth the effort, and is a reminder that Wiccan practice isn't limited to candles, athames and cauldrons.

When we've made a conscious decision to bring our spirituality into our everyday lives, our entire existences considerably brighten. Wicca, after all, consists of reverence of the sources of everything that exists. I hardly think that the Goddess' and God's teachings are relevant solely on the Sabbats and Esbats.

We needn't change our entire lives to live within Wicca's framework. We don't have to abandon our families and move to Tibet, or spend all day, every day, in ritual. Often, the greatest changes that need to be made are mental, not physical. A truly positive outlook ruled by 'harm none' is an excellent first step in Wiccan living. It can also be quite challenging (especially when driving in rush-hour traffic or vying for a parking space).

There are no failures. When we get angry, we can remember that the deities have such emotions within them as well (though we don't spend time invoking these particular divine aspects). If a temporary lapse of consciousness allows us to litter, we needn't ask forgiveness of anyone but ourselves as we bend to retrieve that candy wrapper.

There are two things to remember when attempting to live a Wiccan life: there's nothing that we can do that, mythologically speaking, the deities haven't done. (They're unshockable.) The Goddess and God understand everything; nothing is beyond their ken.

Second, we're not here on this planet to ask forgiveness of our deities. This would be similar to apologizing to our stylist or barber because our hair just keeps on growing. The Earth is a classroom. We're the students. Karma, life, ourselves, others and the Goddess and God are the teachers, and we can't always know the answers. Mistakes are a part of human life. Apologize all you want, if you wish, but learn from your mistakes and, if possible or necessary, correct them. Forgive yourself and move on.

Once we've learned the basics of Wiccan beliefs and practices, living our religion is, logically, the next step. How we allow it to affect our lives is completely up to us.

I've written this book as a guide not only to Wiccan practice, but to Wiccan life. Still, its contents are merely ideas and suggestions. Each of us has to find the perfect path. May the Goddess and God assist you in this quest.

Blessed Be.

GLOSSARY

This is both a glossary and a review of general Wiccan ritual techniques and beliefs. I've tried to make the glossary as non-sectarian and universal as possible. Many Wiccan traditions possess specific concepts concerning some of these terms and will disagree with me. That's fine. Italicized terms within the body of each entry refer to other, related entries in the glossary.

Athame: A Wiccan *Ritual* knife. It may possess a double-edged blade and a black handle. The athame is used to direct *Personal Power* during ritual workings. It is seldom used for actual, physical cutting. The term is of obscure origin; has many variant spellings among Wiccans, and an even greater variety of pronunciations. British and American East Coast Wiccans may pronounce it as "Ah-THAM-ee" (to rhyme with "whammy"); I was first taught to say "ATH-ah-may" and, later, "Ah-THAW-may."

Balefire: A fire laid and lit for magical or religious purposes, usually outdoors. Balefires are tradition adjuncts to Wiccan *Ritual* on *Yule*, *Beltane* and *Midsummer*.

Bane: That which destroys life; is not useful, is poisonous, destructive or evil.

Baneful: See *Bane:*

B.C.E.: Before Common Era; the non-religious equivalent of B.C.

Beltane: A Wiccan religious festival, observed on April 30th, that celebrates the burgeoning fertility of the Earth (and, for some Wiccans, the wedding of the *Goddess* and the *God*). Synonyms include May Eve, Roodmas, Walpurgis Night and Cethsamhain

Besom: Broom.

Boline: The white-handled knife, used in Wiccan and magic Ritual, for practical purposes such as cutting herbs or piercing pomegranates Compare with *Athame*.

Blessing: The act of conferring positive *Energy* upon a person, place or thing. It's a spiritual or religious practice.

Book of Shadows, The: A collection of Wiccan *Ritual* information that usually includes religious rituals, magic and advice. There are many Books of Shadows; there is no one correct Book of Shadows.

Cakes and Wine: Also known as Cakes and Ale, this is a simple ritual meal shared with the *Goddess* and *God*, usually within the *Circle*, near the completion of a religious ritual. Such ritual meals predate Christianity.

C.E.: Common Era; the non-religious equivalent of A.D.

Censer: A heat-proof container in which incense is smoldered during ritual. An incense burner. Usually associated, in Wicca, with the *Element* of Air.

Charging: See *Empowering*.

Circle, Magic: A sphere constructed to *Personal Power* in which Wiccan rituals are usually enacted. The area inside the circle is seen as being common ground on which Wiccans and their Deities can meet. The term refers to the circle that marks the sphere's penetration of the ground, for it extends both above and below it. The magic circle is created through *Magic*.

Circle Casting: The process of moving positive energy from the body and forming it into a large, non-physical sphere of power in which Wiccan rituals usually occur. Circle castings usually begin each Wiccan ritual. The process is also known as 'laying the circle' and 'creating sacred space', among other terms.

Clockwise: The traditional form of movement in positive magic and in Wiccan ritual. (If you're standing facing a tree, move to your left and walk in a circle around it. That's clockwise motion.) Also known as Deosil movement.

Conscious Mind: The analytical, materially-based, rational half of our consciousness. Compare with *Psychic Mind*.

Consecration: The act of conferring sanctity. In Wicca, tools used in religious and magical rites are consecrated with Energy during specific rituals.

Coven: A group of Wiccans, usually initiatory and led by one or two leaders, that gathers together for religious and magical workings. Most covens operate within a specific Wiccan *Tradition*.

Craft, The: Wicca.

Deosil: See *Clockwise*.

Divine Power: The unmanifested, pure energy that exists within the *Goddess* and *God*. The life force; the ultimate source of all things. It is this energy that Wiccans contact during *Ritual*. Compare with *Earth Power* and *Personal Power*.

Divination: The magical art of discovering the unknown by interpreting random patterns or symbols. Sometimes incorrectly referred to as 'fortune-telling'.

Earth Power: That energy which exists within stones, herbs, flames, wind, water and other natural objects. It is manifested *Divine Power* and can be utilized during *magic* to create needed change. Compare with *Personal Power*.

Elements, The: Earth, Air, Fire and Water. These four essences are the building blocks of the universe, and ancient magical sources of *Energy*.

Empowering: The act of moving Energy into an object.

Energy: A general term for the currently unmeasurable (but real) power that exists within all natural objects and beings— including our own bodies. It is used in *Folk Magic*. See also *Personal Power*.

Esbat: A Wiccan ritual occurring on any day other than the eight *Sabbats* Esbats are often held on full moons, which are dedicated to the *Goddess*

Folk Magic: The practice of magic utilizing *Personal Power*, in conjunction with natural *Tools*, in a non-religious framework, to cause positive change.

Goal, The: See *Intent*.

God, The: Generally, in Wicca, the God is the male principle; the perfect complement to the *Goddess.* He's often identified with the sun; with deserts and forests, and with wild animals. Some see Him as the Lord of Death and Resurrection. In the eight *Sabbats* the Wiccans celebrate His birth, maturity, union with the Goddess and His death. The God is not to be confused with common Christian conception of 'God'.

Goddess, The: There are as many definitions of the Goddess as there are Wiccans. Generally, She's seen as the creatress of the universe; the unfaltering, ultimate source of fertility, wisdom, love, compassion, healing and power. Often associated with the Moon, the seas and the Earth in Wiccan thought, the Goddess has been worshipped in many religions across the globe and throughout time.

Handfasting: Within Wicca, a ritual joining of two human beings in a bond of love, and before the *Goddess* and *God.*

Herb: Virtually any plant used in magic.

High Priest: In group Wicca, either one of two visible leaders of a *Coven;* a man who co-leads the rituals, or a man who has reached a certain level of proficiency, achievement and wisdom. The term usually denotes a man who has received not one but several initiations.

High Priestess: A highly experienced leader of a *Coven;* the woman who leads or co-leads the rituals, or a woman who has reached a certain level of Wiccan proficiency, achievement and wisdom. The term usually denotes a woman who has received not one but several initiations.

Imbolc: A Wiccan religious festival celebrated on February 1st or 2nd that marks the first stirring of Spring.

Intent: In magic, the goal of the working.

Initiation: A process whereby an individual is introduced or admitted into a group, interest, skill or religion. Initiations may be *Ritual* occasions, or may spontaneously occur.

Invocation: An appeal or petition to a higher power (or powers). Invocation is a method of establishing conscious ties with those aspects of the Goddess and God that dwell within us. Invocation seemingly invites Them to appear. In actuality, invocation simply makes us newly aware of Their presence.

Law of Three, The: A Wiccan belief that our actions, both positive and negative, will be returned to us three-fold.

Litha: The Summer Solstice, a Wiccan religious festival and a traditional time for magic. Also known as Midsummer.

'Luck, Good': An individual's ability to make timely, correct decisions, to perform correct actions and to place herself or himself in positive situations. 'Bad luck' stems from ignorance and an unwillingness to accept self-responsibility.

Lughnasadh: A Wiccan religious festival celebrated on August 1st that marks the first harvest.

Magic: The movement of natural (yet subtle) *Energies* to manifest positive, needed change. Magic is the process of rousing energy, giving it purpose (through *Visualization*), and releasing it to create a change. This is a natural (not supernatural) practice.

Magic Circle: See *Circle*.

Mabon: A Wiccan religious festival celebrated on the Autumn Equinox that marks the second harvest.

Meditation: Reflection, contemplation, turning inward toward the self or outward toward Deity or nature.

Ostara: A Wiccan festival celebrated on the Spring Solstice that marks the beginning of the return of evident fertility to the Earth.

Pagan: From the Latin *paganus,* a 'country dweller' or 'villager' Today it's used as a general term for followers of Wicca and other polytheistic, magic-embracing religions. Pagans aren't Satanists, dangerous, or evil.

Pentacle: A ritual object (usually a circular piece of wood, clay or metal) upon which a five-pointed star *(Pentagram)* is inscribed, painted or engraved. It represents the *Element* of Earth. The words 'pentagram' and 'pentacle' are not interchangeable in Wiccan use.

Pentagram: An interlaced five-pointed star (one point at its top) that has long been used as a protective device. Today the pentagram is also associated with the *Element* of Earth and with Wicca. It has no evil associations.

Personal Power: That energy which sustains our bodies. We first absorb it from our biological mothers within the womb and, later, from food, water, the moon and sun and other natural objects. We release personal power during stress, exercise, sex, conception and childbirth. *Magic* is usually a movement of personal power for a specific goal.

Power: See *Energy; Personal Power; Earth Power; Divine Power.*

Prayer: The act of focusing one's attention on Deity and engaging in communication. In Wicca, prayer is directed to the *Goddess* and *God* (or sometimes, to one or the other).

Psychic Awareness: The act of being consciously psychic, in which the *Psychic Mind* and the *Conscious Mind* are linked and working in harmony.

Psychic Mind: The subconscious or unconscious mind, in which we receive psychic impulses. The psychic mind is at work when we sleep, dream and meditate.

Reincarnation: The doctrine of rebirth. The process of repeated incarnations in human form to allow evolution of the sexless, ageless human soul. One of the tenets of Wicca.

Rite: See *Ritual*.

Ritual: Ceremony. A specific form of movement, manipulation of objects or inner processes designed to produce desired effects. In religion, ritual is geared toward union with the divine. In *Magic* it allows the magician to move energy toward needed goals. A *Spell* is a magical rite.

Ritual Consciousness:

Runes: Stick-like figures, some of which are remnants of old Teutonic alphabets; others are pictographs. These symbols are once again being widely used in all forms of *Magic*.

Sabbat: A Wiccan religious festival.

Samhain: A Wiccan religious festival celebrated on October 31st, which marks the last harvest and the preparations for Winter.

Scrying: The process of gazing at or into a shiny object, flame or water for the purposes of contacting the *Psychic Mind*.

Solitary Wicca: Wicca practiced, due to either choice or circumstance, by individuals without group support. Compare with *Group Wicca*.

Spell: The mainstay of *Folk Magic*, spells are simply magical rites. They're usually non-religious and often include spoken words.

Tools: A word much-used in Wicca, this term includes both physical objects used to facilitate Wiccan *Ritual* (censers, wands, candles, salt, water and incense) as well as internal process (visualization and concentration, among others). In some forms of *Magic*, this term also refers to stones, herbs, colors and other sources of power utilized in *Spells*.

Tradition, Wiccan: An organized, structured, specific Wiccan subgroup, usually initiatory, often with unique ritual practices. The basis of any tradition is its *Book of Shadows* and specific oral instructions revealed only to initiates. Most traditions are comprised of a number of covens. Most recognize members of other traditions as Wiccans. There are many Wiccan traditions; perhaps the most famous of these is the Gardnerian.

Visualization: The process of forming mental images. Magical visualization consists of forming images of needed goals during *Magic*. It is a function of the *Conscious Mind*.

Wand: One of the ritual *Tools* used in Wicca, the wand is an instrument of *Invocation*, usually utilized to call upon the *Goddess* and the *God*.

Widdershins: Counter-clockwise ritual motion. Compare with *Clockwise*.

Wicca: A contemporary *Pagan* religion with spiritual roots in the earliest expressions of reverence of nature as a manifestation of the divine. Wicca views Deity as *Goddess* and *God;* thus it is polytheistic. It also embraces the practice of *Magic* and accepts reincarnation. Religious festivals are held in observance of the Full Moon and other astronomical (and agricultural) phenomena. It has no associations with Satanism.

Wiccan: Of or relating to *Wicca.*

Witch: Anciently, a European practitioner of pre-Christian *Folk Magic,* particularly that relating to herbs, healing, wells, rivers and stones. One who practiced *Witchcraft.* Later, this term's meaning was altered to denote demented, dangerous beings who practiced destructive magic and who threatened Christianity. This latter definition is false. (Some *Wiccans* also use the word to describe themselves.)

Witchcraft: The Craft of the *Witch. Magic,* especially magic utilizing *Personal Power* in conjunction with the energies within stones, herbs, colors and other natural objects. While this does have spiritual overtones, witchcraft, according to this definition, isn't a religion. However, many followers of *Wicca* use this word to denote their religion. (When it is used in this manner, the first 'w' should be uppercase).

Yule: A Wiccan religious festival celebrated on the Winter Solstice that marks the rebirth of the Sun.

ANNOTATED BIBLIOGRAPHY

Many new books have been published in the last few years. Many others are once again in print. Though all of these works will prove to be of value, I certainly don't agree with every single statement contained within them. Read, as always, with discretion.

WICCA

Anderson, Victor H., *Thorns of the Blood Rose*. Edited and introduced by Gwyddion Pendderwen. Nemeton, 1980. (An intriguing collection of Goddess-inspired poetry.)

Bourne, Lois, *Conversations With a Witch*. London: Robert Hale, 1989. (An English Wiccan's life.)

Cabot, Laurie and Tom Cowan, *Power of the Witch: The Earth, The Moon, and The Magical Path to Enlightenment*. New York: Delta, 1989. (An introduction to Wicca and a guide to folk magic.)

Crowley, Vivianne, Wicca: *The Old Religion in the New Age*. Wellingborough (Northamptonshire, England): Aquarian, 1989. (This is one of the few books published to date that include the word 'Wicca' in its title.)

Crowther, Patricia, *Witch Blood! The Diary of a Witch High Priestess*. New York: House of Collectibles, 1974.

Farrar, Stewart, *What Witches Do: The Modern Coven Revealed*. New York: Coward, McCann, and Geoghehan, 1971 (A look at a coven's activities.)

Farrar, Janet and Stewart Farrar, *The Life and Times of a Modern Witch*. Custer (Washington): Phoenix, 1988. (A fine introduction to Wicca.)

Gardner, Gerald, *The Meaning of Witchcraft*. London: 1959. Reprint. London, Aquarian Press, 1971. Reprint. New York: Magickal Childe Publishing, 1984.

Gardner, Gerald, *Witchcraft Today*. New York: Citadel, 1955. Reprint. New York: Magickal Childe Publishing, 1988. (The first book ever published concerning contemporary Wicca.)

Glass, Justine, *Witchcraft, the Sixth Sense and Us*. North Hollywood: Wilshire, 1965. (Photographs.)

Martello, Leo Louis, *Witchcraft: The Old Religion*. Secaucus (New Jersey): University Books, ND.

Valiente, Doreen, *Where Witchcraft Lives*. London: Aquarian Press, 1962. (An early look at British Wicca and Sussex folklore. Charming and enjoyable reading.)

PRACTICAL INSTRUCTIONS

Budapest, Z., *The Holy Book of Women's Mysteries, Part I*. Oakland: The Susan B. Anthony Coven #1, 1979.

Buckland, Raymond, *The Tree: The Complete Book of Saxon Witchcraft*. New York: Weiser, 1974. (Complete guide to a Wiccan tradition.)

Buckland, Raymond, *Buckland's Complete Book of Witchcraft*. St. Paul: Llewellyn Publications, 1986.

Campanelli, Pauline and Dan Campanelli, *Wheel of the Year: Living the Magical Life*. St. Paul: Llewellyn Publications, 1989. (These two Wiccans have created a charming and eminently usable collection of Wiccan, Pagan and magical information and activities for every month of the year. A true delight.)

Crowther, Patricia, *Lid Off The Cauldron: A Handbook for Witches*. London: Robert Hale, 1981. (Another practical guide.)

Farrar, Janet and Stewart Farrar, *Eight Sabbats for Witches*. London: Robert Hale, 1981. (The Sabbat rituals, plus a unique look at the origins of the first Book of Shadows, courtesy of Doreen Valiente.)

Farrar, Janet and Stewart Farrar, *The Witches' Way*: Principles, Rituals and Beliefs of Modern Witchcraft. London: Robert Hale, 1984. (Further revelations concerning Gardner's Book of Shadows and much practical information. Note: This book has been reprinted and bound with the Farrars' Eight Sabbats For Witches by Magickal Childe Publishing; the combined volume is entitled A Witches' Bible Compleat.)

Fitch, Ed, *Magical Rites From the Crystal Well*. St. Paul: Llewellyn Publications, 1984. (Neo-Pagan rituals for every occasion.)

Green, Marian, *A Witch Alone: Thirteen Moons to Master Natural Magic*. London: Aquarian Press, 1991. (An unusual book; each chapter guides the reader through lessons designed to increase her or his magical and Wiccan proficiency. Not entirely Wiccan in focus, but well-crafted, with an obvious British audience in mind.)

K., Amber, *How To Organize a Coven or Magickal Study Group*. Madison (Wisconsin): Circle Publications, 1983. (Explicit guidelines for doing just that.)

Slater, Herman (editor) *A Book of Pagan Rituals* New York Weiser, 1974. (Another collection of rituals drawn from the Pagan Way.)

Slater, Herman (editor) *Pagan Rituals III: Outer Court Training Coven*. New York: Magical Childe Publishing, 1989. (The first part of this book reprints The Witchcraft Fact Book, written by the late Ed Buczynski. The second half contains a complete "outer court" (i.e., non-initiatory) Book of Shadows originally written for students of a Welsh tradition.)

Starhawk, *The Spiral Dance*. San Francisco: Harper and Row, 1979. (The classic guide to Goddess worship.)

Valiente, Doreen, *Witchcraft For Tomorrow*. London: Robert Hale, 1978. (Contains a partial Book of Shadows as well as several chapters covering various aspects of Wicca.)

Valiente, Doreen and Evan Jones, *Witchcraft: A Tradition Renewed*. Custer (Washington): Phoenix. (A curious reconstruction of the rituals and beliefs of Robert Cochrane that, in part, inspired the Regency and 1734 traditions of Witchcraft. Far different from anything else that has ever been published.)

Weinstein, Marion, *Earth Magic: A Dianic Book of Shadows*. New York: Earth Magic Productions, 1980. Reprint. Custer (Washington): Phoenix, 1986. (A unique guide like no others. Not a complete Book of Shadows, perhaps, but certainly fascinating and useful.)

THE GODDESS

Downing, Christine, *The Goddess: Mythological Images of the Feminine*. New York: Crossroad, 1984.

Gimbutas, Marija, *The Goddesses and Gods of Old Europe*. Berkeley: The University of California Press, 1982.

Gimbutas, Marija, *The Language of the Goddess*. San Francisco: Harper & Row, 1989. (A monumental, overwhelming work. Many photographs and illustrations.)

Graves, Robert, *The White Goddess*. New York: Farrar, Straus and Giroux, 1973.

Neumann, Erich, *The Great Mother: An Analysis of the Archetype*. Princeton: Princeton University Press, 1974. (A Jungian approach to the Goddess. This work concludes with 185 pages of photographs of Goddess images.)

Stone, Merlin, *When God Was a Woman*. New York: Dial Press, 1976.

Walker, Barbara, *The Woman's Dictionary of Symbols and Sacred Objects*. San Francisco: Harper & Row, 1988.

Walker, Barbara, *The Woman's Encyclopedia of Myth and Secrets*. San Francisco: Harper & Row, 1983.

WICCAN REFERENCE WORKS

Adler, Margot, *Drawing Down the Moon: Witches, Druids, Goddess-Worshippers, and Other Pagans in America Today*. Revised and Expanded Edition. Boston: Beacon Press, 1986. (This book is must reading, for it provides an overview of contemporary Wicca and Paganism. Photographs.)

Burland, C. A., *Echoes of Magic: A Study of Seasonal Festivals Through the Ages* London : Peter Davies, ND. (An engrossing study of the symbolism of the seasonal festivals [Sabbats] by an expert folklorist. The entire volume is somewhat peculiarly given over to the author's great joy in writing of sexual matters. Still a wonderful source.)

Farrar, Janet and Stewart Farrar, *The Witches' God: Lord of the Dance.* Custer (Washington): Phoenix, 1989. (A book-length look at the God in Wicca. Photographs.)

Farrar, Janet and Stewart Farrar, *The Witches' Goddess.* Custer (Washington): Phoenix, 19??. (Photographs.)

Guiley, Rosemary, *The Encyclopedia of Witches and Witchcraft.* New York: Facts on File, 1989. (A well-researched, sympathetic, encyclopedic work.)

Kelly, Aidan A., *Crafting the Art of Magic: A History of Modern Witchcraft, 1939-1964.* St. Paul: Llewellyn Publications, 1991. (A speculative reconstruction of the creation of modern Wicca.)

Mathers, S. L. MacGregor, (editor and translator), *The Key of Solomon the King.* New York: Weiser, 1972 (Some modern Wiccan rites were partially based on this work. Wicca has also borrowed some symbolism from the Key.)

Valiente, Doreen, *The Rebirth of Witchcraft.* London: Robert Hale, 1989. Reprint. Custer (Washington): Phoenix, 1989. (An important addition to Wicca's recent history; informative and enthralling.)

MAGIC

K., Amber, *True Magick: A Beginner's Guide*. St. Paul: Llewellyn, 1990. (An extremely Wiccan-based introduction to folk magic.)

Howard, Michael, *The Magic of Runes*. New York: Weiser, 1980.

Howard, Michael, *The Runes and Other Magical Alphabets*. New York: Weiser, 1978.

Koch, Rudolph, *The Book of Signs*. New York: Dover, 1955.

Mathers, S. L. MacGregor (editor and translator), *The Key of Solomon The King*. New York: Weiser, 1972.

Pepper, Elizabeth and John Wilcox, *Witches All*. New York: Grosset and Dunlap, 1977. (A collection of folk magic drawn from the popular *Witches' Almanac*, which is once again in annual production.

Tyson, Donald, *Rune Magic*. St. Paul: Llewellyn Publications, 1988.

Valiente, Doreen, *Natural Magic*. New York: St. Martin's Press, 1975.

Weinstein, Marion, *Positive Magic: Occult Self-Help*. New York: Pocket Books, 1978. (A wonderful introduction to magic. An expanded edition has also been published.)

INDEX

Stay in Touch. . .

Llewellyn publishes hundreds of books on your favorite subjects

On the following pages you will find listed some books now available on related subjects. Your local bookstore stocks most of these and will stock new Llewellyn titles as they become available. We urge your patronage.

Order by Phone

Call toll-free within the U.S. and Canada, 1–800–THE MOON. In Minnesota call **(612) 291–1970**. We accept Visa, MasterCard, and American Express.

Order by Mail

Send the full price of your order (MN residents add 7% sales tax) in U.S. funds to:

Llewellyn Worldwide
P.O. Box 64383, Dept. L184-9
St. Paul, MN 55164–0383, U.S.A.

Postage and Handling

◆ $4.00 for orders $15.00 and under
◆ $5.00 for orders over $15.00
◆ No charge for orders over $100.00

We ship UPS in the continental United States. We cannot ship to P.O. boxes. Orders shipped to Alaska, Hawaii, Canada, Mexico, and Puerto Rico will be sent first-class mail.

International orders: Airmail—add freight equal to price of each book to the total price of order, plus $5.00 for each non-book item (audiotapes, etc.). Surface mail—Add $1.00 per item.

Allow 4–6 weeks delivery on all orders. Postage and handling rates subject to change.

Group Discounts

We offer a 20% quantity discount to group leaders or agents. You must order a minimum of 5 copies of the same book to get our special quantity price.

Free Catalog

Get a free copy of our color catalog, *New Worlds of Mind and Spirit*. Subscribe for just $10.00 in the United States and Canada ($20.00 overseas, first class mail). Many bookstores carry *New Worlds*—ask for it!

EARTH POWER
Techniques of Natural Magic
by Scott Cunningham

Magick is the art of working with the forces of Nature to bring about necessary and desired, changes. The forces of Nature—expressed through Earth, Air, Fire and Water—are our "spiritual ancestors" who paved the way for our emergence from the prehistoric seas of creation. Attuning to and working with these energies in magick not only lends you the power to affect changes in your life, it also allows you to sense your own place in the larger scheme of Nature. Using the "Old Ways" enables you to live a better life and to deepen your understanding of the world. The tools and powers of magick are around you, waiting to be grasped and utilized. This book gives you the means to put Magick into your life, shows you how to make and use the tools, and gives you spells for every purpose

0-87542-121-0, 176 pgs., 5¼ x 8, illus., softcover $9.95

EARTH, AIR, FIRE & WATER
More Techniques of Natural Magic
by Scott Cunningham

A water-smoothed stone . . . The wind . . . A candle's flame . . . A pool of water. These are the age-old tools of natural magic. Born of the Earth, possessing inner power, they await only our touch and intention to bring them to life. The four Elements are the ancient powerhouses of magic. Using their energies, we can transform ourselves, our lives and our worlds. Tap into the marvelous powers of the natural world with these rites, spells and simple rituals that you can do easily and with a minimum of equipment. This book includes more than 75 spells, rituals and ceremonies; detailed instructions for designing your own magical spells; instills a sense of wonder concerning our planet and our lives; and promotes a natural, positive practice that anyone can successfully perform.

0-897542-131-8, 240 pgs., 6 x 9, illus., softcover $9.95

CUNNINGHAM'S ENCYCLOPEDIA OF
CRYSTAL, GEM & METAL MAGIC
by Scott Cunningham

Here you will find the most complete information anywhere on the magical qualities of more than 100 crystals and gemstones as well as several metals. The information for each crystal, gem or metal includes: its related energy, planetary rulership, magical element, deities, Tarot Card, and the magical powers that each is believed to possess. Also included is a complete description of their uses for magical purposes. The classic on the subject.

0-87542-126-1, 240 pgs., 6 x 9, illus., color plates, softcover $14.95

WICCA
A Guide for the Solitary Practitioner
by Scott Cunningham

Wicca is a book of life, and how to live magically, spiritually, and wholly attuned with Nature. Cunningham presents Wicca as it is today: a gentle, Earth-oriented religion dedicated to the Goddess and God. This book fulfills a need for a practical guide to solitary Wicca—a need which no previous book has fulfilled. Here is a positive, practical introduction to the religion of Wicca, designed so that any interested person can learn to practice the religion alone, anywhere in the world. It presents Wicca honestly and clearly, without the pseudo-history that permeates other books. It shows that Wicca is a vital, satisfying part of twentieth century life.

This book presents the theory and practice of Wicca from an individual's perspective. The section on the Standing Stones Book of Shadows contains solitary rituals for the Esbats and Sabbats. This book, based on the author's nearly two decades of Wiccan practice, presents an eclectic picture of various aspects of this religion. Exercises designed to develop magical proficiency, a self-dedication ritual, herb, crystal and rune magic, recipes for Sabbat feasts, are included in this excellent book.

0-87542-118-0, 240 pgs., 6 x 9, illus., softcover $9.95

CUNNINGHAM'S ENCYCLOPEDIA OF MAGICAL HERBS
by Scott Cunningham

This is the most comprehensive source of herbal data for magical uses ever printed! Almost every one of the over 400 herbs are illustrated, making this a great source for herb identification. For each herb you will also find: magical properties, planetary rulerships, genders, associated deities, folk and Latin names and much more. To make this book even easier to use, it contains a folk name cross reference, and all of the herbs are fully indexed.

Like all of Cunningham's books, this one does not require you to use complicated rituals or expensive magical paraphernalia. Instead, it shares with you the intrinsic powers of the herbs. Thus, you will be able to discover which herbs, by their very nature, can be used for luck, love, success, money, divination, astral projection, safety, psychic self-defense and much more. Besides being interesting and educational it is also fun, and fully illustrated with unusual woodcuts from old herbals. This book has rapidly become the classic in its field. It enhances books such as 777 and is a must for all Wiccans.

0-87542-122-9, 336 pgs., 6 x 9, illus., softcover $14.95

MAGICAL HERBALISM
The Secret Craft of the Wise
by Scott Cunningham

Certain plants are prized for the special range of energies they possess. *Magical Herbalism* unites the powers of plants and man to produce, and direct, change in accord with human will and desire. This is the Magic of amulets and charms, sachets and herbal pillows, incenses, scented oils, simples, infusions and anointments.

This is Magic that is beautiful and natural—a Craft of Hand and Mind merged with the Power and Glory of Nature: a special kind that does not use the medicinal powers of herbs, but rather the subtle vibrations and scents that touch the psychic centers and stir the astral field in which we live to work at the causal level behind the material world. This is the Magic of Enchantment . . . of word and gesture to shape the images of mind and channel the energies of the herbs. It is a Magic for everyone: the herbs and tools are easily obtained. This book includes step-by-step guidance to the preparation of herbs with simple rituals and spells for every purpose.
0-87542-120-2, 260 pgs., 5-¼ x 8, illus., softcover   **$9.95**

MAGICAL AROMATHERAPY
The Power of Scent
by Scott Cunningham

Scent magic has a rich, colorful history. Today, in the shadow of the next century, there is much we can learn from the simple plants that grace our planet. Most have been used for countless centuries. The energies still vibrate within their aromas.

Scott Cunningham has now combined the current knowledge of the physiological and psychological effects of natural fragrances with the ancient art of magical perfumery. In writing this book, he drew on extensive experimentation and observation, research into 4,000 years of written records, and the wisdom of respected aromatherapy practitioners. *Magical Aromatherapy* contains a wealth of practical tables of aromas of the seasons, days of the week, the planets, and zodiac; use of essential oils with crystals; synthetic and genuine oils and hazardous essential oils. It also contains a handy appendix of aromatherapy organizations and distributors of essential oils and dried plant products.
0-87542-129-6, 224 pgs., mass market, illus.   **$3.95**

THE MAGICAL HOUSEHOLD
Empower Your Home with Love,
Protection, Health and Happiness
by Scott Cunningham and David Harrington

Whether your home is a small apartment or a palatial mansion, you want it to be something special. Now it can be with *The Magical Household*. Learn how to make your home more than just a place to live. Turn it into a place of security, life, fun and magic. Here you will not find the complex magic of the ceremonial magician. Rather, you will learn simple, quick and effective magical spells that use nothing more than common items in your house: furniture, windows, doors, carpet, pets, etc. You will learn to take advantage of the intrinsic power and energy that is already in your home, waiting to be tapped. You will learn to make magic a part of your life. The result is a home that is safeguarded from harm and a place which will bring you happiness, health and more.

0-87542-124-5, 208 pgs., 5-¼ x 8, illus., softcover   **$9.95**

THE MAGIC OF FOOD
Legends, Lore & Spells
by Scott Cunningham

Foods are storehouses of natural energies. Choosing specific foods, properly preparing them, eating with a magical goal in mind: these are the secrets of *The Magic in Food*, an age-old method of taking control of your life through your diet.

Though such exotic dishes as bird's-nest soup and saffron bread are included in this book, you'll find many old friends: peanut butter and jelly sandwiches ... scrambled eggs ... tofu ... beer. We've consumed them for years, but until we're aware of the energies contained within them, foods offer little more than nourishment and pleasure.

You'll learn the mystic qualities of everyday dishes, their preparation (if any) and the simple method of calling upon their powers. The author has included numerous magical diets, each designed to create a specific change within its user: increased health and happiness, deeper spirituality, enhanced sexual relations, protection, psychic awareness, success, love, prosperity—all through the hidden powers of food.

0-87542-130-X, 384 pgs., 6 x 9, illus., color plates, softcover **$14.95**

BUCKLAND'S COMPLETE BOOK OF WITCHCRAFT
by Raymond Buckland

Here is the most complete resource to the study and practice of modern, non-denominational Wicca. This is a lavishly illustrated, self-study course for the solitary or group. Included are rituals; exercises for developing psychic talents; information on all major "sects" of the Craft; sections on tools, beliefs, dreams, meditations, divination, herbal lore, healing, ritual clothing and much, much more. This book unites theory and practice into a comprehensive course designed to help you develop into a practicing Witch, one of the "Wise Ones." It is written by Ray Buckland, a very famous and respected authority on Witchcraft who first came public with the Old Religion in the United States. Large format with workbook-type exercises, profusely illustrated and full of music and chants. Takes you from A to Z in the study of Witchcraft.

Traditionally, there are three degrees of advancement in most Wiccan traditions. When you have completed studying this book, you will be the equivalent of a Third-Degree Witch. Even those who have practiced Wicca for years find useful information in this book, and many covens are using this for their textbook. If you want to become a Witch, or if you merely want to find out what Witchcraft is really about, you will find no better book than this.

0-87542-050-8, 272 pgs., 8-½ x 11, illus., softcover $14.95

ANCIENT WAYS
Reclaiming the Pagan Tradition
by Pauline Campanelli, illus. by Dan Campanelli

Ancient Ways is filled with magick and ritual that you can perform every day to capture the spirit of the seasons. It focuses on the celebration of the Sabbats of the Old Religion by giving you practical things to do while anticipating the sabbat rites, and helping you harness the magical energy for weeks afterward. The wealth of seasonal rituals and charms are drawn from ancient sources but are easily performed with materials readily available.

Learn how to look into your previous lives at Yule . . . at Beltane, discover the places where you are most likely to see faeries . . . make special jewelry to wear for your Lammas Celebrations . . . for the special animals in your life, and paint a charm of protection at Midsummer. Most Pagans and Wiccans feel that the Sabbat rituals are all too brief and wish for the magick to continue longer. *Ancient Ways* can help you reclaim your own traditions and heighten the feeling of real magick.

0-87542-090-7, 256 pgs., 7 x 10, illus., softcover $14.95